Charles Dickens

Charles Dickens

An Introduction

JENNY HARTLEY

OXFORD
UNIVERSITY PRESS

Great Clarendon Street, Oxford, OX2 6DP,
United Kingdom

Oxford University Press is a department of the University of Oxford.
It furthers the University's objective of excellence in research, scholarship,
and education by publishing worldwide. Oxford is a registered trade mark of
Oxford University Press in the UK and in certain other countries

First Edition published in 2016

Impression: 1

Published in the United States of America by Oxford University Press
198 Madison Avenue, New York, NY 10016, United States of America

British Library Cataloguing in Publication Data
Data available

Library of Congress Control Number: 2016942476

ISBN 978-0-19-878816-4

Printed in Great Britain by
Clays Ltd, St Ives plc

CONTENTS

LIST OF ILLUSTRATIONS

NOTE ON EDITIONS

Quotations from *Sketches by Boz* and Dickens's journalism are taken from *Dickens' Journalism*, ed. Michael Slater and John Drew, 4 vols. (J. M. Dent, 1994–2000). Quotations from Dickens's letters are taken from *The Letters of Charles Dickens*, ed. Graham Storey et al, 12 vols. (Pilgrim Edition, Clarendon Press, 1965–2002). Quotations from Dickens's public speeches are taken from *The Speeches of Charles Dickens: A Complete Edition*, ed. K. J. Fielding (Harvester Wheatsheaf, 1988). Quotations from the following works by Dickens are taken from the Oxford Clarendon Press editions where available, otherwise from the Oxford World's Classics editions, and are reproduced by permission of Oxford University Press.

A Christmas Carol, ed. Robert Douglas-Fairhurst (Oxford University Press, 2006)

A Tale of Two Cities, ed. Andrew Sanders (Oxford University Press, 2008)

Barnaby Rudge, ed. Clive Hurst (Oxford University Press, 2003)

Bleak House, ed. Stephen Gill (Oxford University Press, 1996)

David Copperfield, ed. Nina Burgis (Oxford University Press, 1981)

Dombey and Son, ed. Alan Horsman (Oxford University Press, 1974)
Edwin Drood, ed. Margaret Cardwell (Oxford University Press, 1972)
Great Expectations, ed. Margaret Cardwell (Oxford University Press, 1993)
Hard Times, ed. Paul Schlicke (Oxford University Press, 2008)
Little Dorrit, ed. Harvey Peter Sucksmith (Oxford University Press, 1979)
Martin Chuzzlewit, ed. Margaret Cardwell (Oxford University Press, 1982)
Nicholas Nickleby, ed. Paul Schlicke (Oxford University Press, 1990)
Oliver Twist, ed. Kathleen Tillotson (Oxford University Press, 1966)
Our Mutual Friend, ed. Michael Cotsell (Oxford University Press, 2008)
Pickwick Papers, ed. James Kinsley (Oxford University Press, 1986)
The Old Curiosity Shop, ed. Elizabeth M. Brennan (Oxford University Press, 1997)

1

More

Let us begin with someone you may already have met: nine-year-old Oliver Twist in the workhouse.

> Boys have generally excellent appetites. Oliver Twist and his companions suffered the tortures of slow starvation for three months; at last they got so voracious and wild with hunger, that one boy: who was tall for his age, and hadn't been used to that sort of thing, (for his father had kept a small cook's shop): hinted darkly to his companions, that unless he had another basin of gruel *per diem*, he was afraid he might some night happen to eat the boy who slept next him, who happened to be a weakly youth of tender age. He had a wild, hungry, eye; and they implicitly believed him. A council was held; lots were cast who should walk up to the master after supper that evening, and ask for more; and it fell to Oliver Twist.
>
> The evening arrived; the boys took their places. The master, in his cook's uniform, stationed himself at the copper; his pauper assistants ranged themselves behind him; the gruel was served out; and a long grace was said over the short commons. The gruel disappeared; the boys whispered each other, and winked at Oliver; while his next neighbours nudged him. Child as he was, he was desperate with hunger, and reckless with misery. He rose from the table; and advancing

> to the master, basin and spoon in hand, said: somewhat alarmed at his own temerity:
>
> 'Please, sir, I want some more.'
>
> The master was a fat, healthy man; but he turned very pale. He gazed in stupefied astonishment on the small rebel for some seconds; and then clung for support to the copper. The assistants were paralysed with wonder; the boys with fear.
>
> 'What!' said the master at length, in a faint voice.
>
> 'Please, sir,' replied Oliver, 'I want some more.'
>
> (Chapter 2)

This is one of literature's best-known scenes, a perfect image of innocence protesting against injustice. Oliver asking for more has done so much on behalf of so many—social causes, opportunities for adaptation, entertainment and commerce—that it looks like a good place to start exploring the extraordinary phenomenon of Charles Dickens. What clues does the scene have for us, and what happens when we track it back to its first appearance?

Asking for More

The passage turns out to be more than the simple cry of hunger. Social campaigners can write indignant pleas for reform; what Dickens gives us is black comedy. This is satire as savage cannibalistic hilarity. Dickens enjoys the tall boy threatening to eat the 'weakly youth'. The detail of his father's small cook's shop splices the mundane with the comic gothic of the absent-minded ogre 'afraid he might some night happen to eat' the boy next to him. Different languages thread through the passage to electrify it. The Latin *per diem* (daily) comes from the Poor Law regulations and alludes to the mingy allowances stipulated there; the boys' 'council' recalls the real councils and organizations which should be caring for them. The elegantly balanced formal wordplay of the 'long grace . . . over the short commons' temporarily conceals—as the people who use this kind of language would prefer—the blunt fact that these children are not being given enough to eat. The narrator seems kindly with his observation that 'Boys have generally excellent appetites', but his diction can strike a distanced note, describing Oliver as 'somewhat alarmed by his own temerity'. We have to translate this into the child's own words and emotions of being scared, and that helps to bond us with the child.

The different languages and frames of reference, the narrator, the threatening boys, Oliver, the institutional voices of workhouse and (absent) state: Dickens puts us on our toes as we switch from one to the other. And all of this we keep running in our heads while we rush on to see what will happen next. But we are also invited to see the tableau as a performance, set up and prepared for dramatically: 'lots were cast who should walk up'. It is a scene carefully choreographed visually. We watch as everyone gets into position: the boys moved into their places, the fat master by the pot with the gruel in it, pauper assistants behind him. We know beforehand that Oliver is going to speak, but not exactly what he is going to say, so we wait with anticipation. His famous words combine the polite 'Please, sir'—here is a boy who knows his place and his manners—with the firm assertion of not 'may I' or 'can I' but 'I want'. The sentence starts in deference and ends in rebellion.

This then is the iconic moment; let us see what more there is to it and around it. Dickens himself made sure there was more by having it illustrated (see Figure 1). George Cruikshank brings out the scariness with his crew of cadaverous boys licking their bowls, sucking their spoons and fingers just as Dickens describes. The tall boy hovers ghoulishly at the back, and what are those weird shadows behind him? Oliver may be a meek and pale little boy, but Dickens conspicuously counts him in as one of the band made 'voracious and wild' by hunger. Oliver himself is 'desperate' and 'reckless'. The starving boys, like Dickens's prose, burst out in energy.

When Dickens wrote the Oliver scene in January 1837, he was just short of his twenty-fifth birthday. It was a whirlwind time for him. The passage comes from the first instalment of *Oliver Twist*, which was not his first novel but was the first one of which he was in charge. His first novel, *The Posthumous Papers of the Pickwick Club,* was based on a commission from publishers Chapman & Hall, and Dickens was still writing it. To begin with it sold poorly. The print run for the second instalment was cut from 1,000 to 500. But with the introduction of Cockney servant Sam Weller and his aphorism for every occasion, sales took off and soared to 40,000. It was not, though, just about Pickwick on the page. From very early on, 'in less than six months from the appearance of the first number', noted Percy Fitzgerald, who contributed to Dickens's magazines, and was so impressed that he wrote a book on *The History of Pickwick*, 'the whole reading world was talking about it... Pickwick chintzes figured in linen-drapers' windows, and

Figure 1 *'Oliver asking for more', by George Cruikshank, 1837. Cruikshank was one of the most famous illustrators and caricaturists of the time.*

Weller corduroys in breeches-makers' advertisements.' Brand merchandising had found its first hit.

Dickens had been engaged to provide the text to accompany illustrations about a sporting club. He knew little about sport but he liked the idea of a club, and, as he said in his Preface to the 1847 edition, 'I thought of Mr Pickwick'.

Named after its founder, the Pickwickians enjoy themselves on outings from London; they get into embarrassing scrapes; food and/or drink feature on practically every page. If there is little plot to speak of until its second half, the book is unified by its characters, its humour and jokes, and its pervading mood: 'general benevolence was one of the leading features of the Pickwickian theory' (Chapter 2). It sounded like fun, and readers wanted to join in. Pickwick Clubs instantly sprang up 'all over the kingdom', according to Fitzgerald. Some of them flourish to this day.

The Dickens bandwagon was starting to roll. Well before *Pickwick* had finished its run, imitations and rip-offs were crowding the booksellers. *The Posthumous Papers of the Cadger Club*, *Sam Weller's Favourite Song Book*, *The Pickwick Comic Almanac*, and many many more—'literally endless... variations on the one Pickwick note', commented Fitzgerald. What we see with Dickens's first novel, then, is the spontaneous creation of a whole new dimension of reader interaction and participation. More to Dickens than the books: this is what distinguishes Dickens as a writer throughout his career and from his day until our own. His unique gift to the world has been a club for all who read his books, for all who watch the adaptations on film and television, and for anyone who wants to come to the party. This virtual club opened its doors in 1836, and they have never closed.

Buoyed by the success of *Pickwick*, Dickens felt he was in the driving seat. 'I think I have hit on a capital notion for myself', he wrote about his first ideas for *Oliver Twist*. But he was still writing *Pickwick*, which continued until the autumn of 1837, so he was writing two novels at once—both coming out in monthly instalments, usually of two or three chapters each time. He had also just started to edit a new monthly magazine, *Bentley's Miscellany*. That meant finding contributors, and cutting and 'touching up' their work. 'Dr Milligen's paper . . . has cost me three hours this morning', grumbles Dickens, and already objecting loudly to interference from the publisher Bentley. He was perpetually rearranging terms with the Burlington Street brigand, as he called him—eight times over the next two years. He had agreed to supply sixteen pages of his own writing for the magazine each month, and the first instalment of *Oliver Twist* appears in the second number. It was probably intended to initiate a series of sketches rather than a novel, but Dickens soon spotted the potential. 'Have you seen Oliver Twist yet?' he wrote to Bentley after the first instalment. 'I have taken a great fancy to him—I hope he deserves it.' Improvising to begin with, Dickens could see that these sketches could grow into a novel. But his instalments often fell short of the sixteen pages, so he had to contribute extra bits and pieces of journalism. Over-commitment, we might think—but the energy which sparks the *Oliver Twist* boys to rebellion and crackles through the novel is the lifeblood which surges through Dickens at his best. 'Invention, thank God, seems the easiest thing in the world', he once wrote to his friend John Forster.

He was also working on a farce to be produced on stage, and juggling his dealings with his two publishers, Bentley and Chapman & Hall, alongside negotiations with a third. John Macrone had published Dickens's early journalism as *Sketches by Boz*, and was now cashing in on the *Pickwick* success with a second series of *Sketches*. 'Macrone has driven me so hard', Dickens told Bentley; and to Macrone, Dickens was also contracted to write a three-volume novel, *Gabriel Vardon, the Locksmith of London*, to be delivered between May and November 1836, unstarted and already overdue (it would eventually appear as *Barnaby Rudge* in 1841).

The beginning of 1837, then, saw Dickens with three publications coming out at once, plus a revival of his comic opera *The Village Coquettes*. He was the talk of the town, his name everywhere. At *The Village Coquettes* the audience, according to one reviewer, 'screamed for Boz'. Others were more sceptical. 'The fact is,' pronounced the *Quarterly Review*, 'Mr Dickens writes too often and too fast.... He has risen like a rocket, and he will come down like the stick.' But for the time being the Dickens rocket was rising unimpeded.

In addition to all this writing, editing, and dealings with publishers, there was a hectic family and social life to maintain. The month that saw the birth of little Oliver also saw the birth of Dickens's own first child. His wife Catherine was 'in a very low and alarming state'; he was, he said, 'the only person who could prevail upon her' to eat. But this did not keep him home too much. This was the month he was elected to the Garrick Club, a sign that he now belonged to the London artistic and theatrical set, at the heart of the social and public life of the city. He was also forging his lifelong friendship with John Forster, who would act as confidant and sounding board. It is not surprising to find him complaining of 'violent' headaches and taking 'as much medicine as would confine an ordinary-sized horse to his stall for a week'. Dickens never did anything by halves.

More to *Oliver Twist* than Oliver

There is, of course, more to the novel than the vulnerable child asking for more. Oliver was not the only character to leap from its pages and enjoy a flourishing afterlife beyond the book. The Artful Dodger is introduced as 'one of the queerest-looking boys that Oliver had ever seen'. He is Oliver's age, but with 'all the airs and manners of a man'.

> His hat was stuck on the top of his head so lightly, that it threatened to fall off every moment; and would have done so, very often, if the wearer had not had a knack of every now and then giving his head a sudden twitch: which brought it back to its old place again. He wore a man's coat, which reached nearly to his heels. He had turned the cuffs back, half-way up his arm, to get his hands out of the sleeves: apparently with the ultimate view of thrusting them into the pockets of his corduroy trousers; for there he kept them. He was, altogether, as roystering and swaggering a young gentleman as ever stood four feet six, or something less, in his bluchers [boots].
>
> (Chapter 8)

Dickens does the Dodger with clothes, with jauntiness, and with friendship. '"Hullo! my covey, what's the row?"' are his first words to Oliver, who has been on the road for seven days and is nearly dead with hunger and fatigue. '"Up with you on your pins"', he tells Oliver, and buys him food and drink. He is the boy with spirit. As with hats, so for life: he has the knack, he has style. He is a thief, so he cannot go unpunished, but his swagger is allowed to sparkle undimmed at his trial for pick-pocketing. This is the Dodger's finest hour, and Dickens presents him as if he is in charge of the whole event, another performance moment. He 'desired the jailer to communicate "the names of them two old files as was on the bench," which so tickled the spectators'—and the jailers and court officials too, that the whole court is laughing 'heartily' throughout the show, with the Dodger as actor-manager.

> 'Oh! you know me, do you?' cried the Artful [to the jailer] making a note of the statement. 'Wery good. That's a case of deformation of character, any way.'
>
> Here there was another laugh, and another cry of silence.
>
> 'Now then, where are the witnesses?' said the clerk.
>
> 'Ah! that's right,' added the Dodger. 'Where are they? I should like to see 'em.'
>
> This wish was immediately gratified, for a policeman stepped forward who had seen the prisoner attempt the pocket of an unknown gentleman in a crowd, and indeed take a handkerchief therefrom, which, being a very old one, he deliberately put back again, after trying it on his own countenance.
>
> (Chapter 43)

This is crime as play, a criminal trial as show; but with a satirical twist at the close when Dickens has the Dodger deliver the final verdict.

> 'I never see such an out-and-out young wagabond, your worship,' observed the officer with a grin. 'Do you mean to say anything, you young shaver?'
>
> 'No,' replied the Dodger, 'not here, for this ain't the shop for justice; besides which, my attorney is a-breakfasting this morning with the Wice President of the House of Commons; but I shall have something to say elsewhere, and so will he,

> and so will a wery numerous and 'spectable circle of acquaintance as'll make them beaks wish they'd never been born, or that they'd got their footmen to hang 'em up to their own hat-pegs, afore they let 'em come out this morning to try it on upon me.'
>
> (Chapter 43)

If the Dodger adds to the absurdity so extravagantly, there is another side of the underworld to bring out: the sinister and foul. This is the medium of the criminal Fagin, another character with a vigorous afterlife. Dickens sets him in the element which has 'engendered' him, the particular London districts and streets which Dickens delights in naming, Whitechapel, Spitalfields, Saffron Hill.

> The mud lay thick upon the stones: and a black mist hung over the streets; the rain fell sluggishly down: and everything felt cold and clammy to the touch. It seemed just the night when it befitted such a being as the Jew, to be abroad. As he glided stealthily along, creeping beneath the shelter of the walls and doorways, the hideous old man seemed like some loathsome reptile, engendered in the slime and darkness through which he moved: crawling forth, by night, in search of some rich offal for a meal.
>
> (Chapter 19)

'Loathsome' though this 'reptile' may be, with what relish Dickens follows him through the slime. But Fagin is not just loathsome reptile; he is also the merry old gent who cooks Oliver his first decent meal and provides conviviality, sausages, and laughs.

This duality, this bifocalism, is a characteristic running throughout Dickens's writing. Contradiction and opposition fire his imagination. As John Carey observes, he sees 'almost everything from two opposed points of view'. This is the vision which shapes one of the most famous opening lines in fiction: 'It was the best of times, it was the worst of times' (*A Tale of Two Cities*). Best and worst. Contradictions and oppositions, extremes and hyperbole. These are the hallmarks of the Dickens style. Exaggeration was, in G. K. Chesterton's view, the essence of the Dickens genius. George Gissing agreed: 'Of course he exaggerated, in all but every page.' For Dickens, more is always more. *Oliver Twist* can and has been taken as social realism (this is what life was like for the poor), but it is realism supercharged and intensified, a hyperrealist universe inhabited by reptiles and cannibals.

Emotions tend to be heightened too. People laugh and cry a lot in Dickens. 'We went up to his room . . . and cried very much', reports David Copperfield on finding Mr Micawber in prison (Chapter 11). Dickens is alert to false criers such as the duplicitous Harold Skimpole in *Bleak House*, who sings a ballad about an orphan peasant boy 'thrown on the wide world'—'a song that always made him cry, he told us' (Chapter 31)—while engaged in betraying a real suffering orphan boy in the next room. Good and bad tears: the hypocrites in *Oliver Twist*, Noah Claypole and Mrs Sowerberry, weep copiously to get their way, while the kindly Mr Brownlow pretends he has not been moved to tears by the sight of the starving Oliver. '"Poor boy, poor boy!" said Mr Brownlow, clearing his throat. "I'm rather hoarse this morning, Mrs Bedwin. I'm afraid I have caught cold."' (Chapter 12). Tears belong to the repertoire of emotional expressiveness condemned by some as sentimentalism; for Dickens this display of affect is a sign of feeling, of worth and humanity.

Adaptable Oliver

From the minute he appeared on the bookstalls, everyone was reading *Oliver*. The young Queen Victoria urged her elderly Prime Minister Lord Melbourne to read it, but he resisted: 'I don't *like* those things; I wish to avoid them; I don't like them in *reality*, and therefore I don't wish them represented.' Lord Melbourne was in the minority. Everyone else wanted more. Before the novel finished its run in *Bentley's Miscellany*, ten adaptations of it had appeared on the London stage. Dickens went to one, and was so disgusted that he lay down on the floor of his box at the theatre. It was on the New York stage by 1839 and in the British Parliament from the 1840s; Oliver asking for more became a staple of House of Commons debates. As with *Pickwick*, pirates, plagiarists, and parodists exploited the opportunity, taking the field with Oliver-type stories by pseudonyms such as Bos and Poz to mimic Dickens's own *nom-de-plume* of Boz. Dickens fumed, but the copyright laws of the day could offer him no protection. Later he would himself make the most of *Oliver*'s dramatic possibilities, adapting the murder of Nancy for one of the public readings he gave from his books. It was a grisly job. 'I have been trying, alone by myself, the Oliver Twist murder', he told a friend in 1863, 'but have got something so horrible out of it that I am afraid to try it in public.' He delayed for six years, before making it the centrepiece of his farewell tour because, he told Forster, he wanted 'to leave behind me the recollection of something very passionate and dramatic'. And he certainly did, thrilling audiences with his sensational performance. 'A contagion of fainting', reported Dickens from Bristol; 'I should think we had from a dozen to twenty ladies borne out, stiff and rigid, at various times.'

Oliver turned out to be an adaptable child, friendly to his legions of adopters. The novel is an interactive text, malleable and porous. Versions and manifestations proliferated; translations multiplied, from Albanian to Vietnamese. Even more arrived at Oliver's door with the invention of cinema at the end of the nineteenth century. The big screen loved Dickens, and *Oliver Twist* in particular. There were nineteen adaptations of the novel in the silent era alone. It was Charlie Chaplin's favourite novel. A workhouse child himself, he re-read *Oliver Twist* throughout his life and wove it into his (and cinema's) first full-length comedy, *The Kid* (1921). More broadly, Dickens's style chimed with how film worked. His reference to the slackening pace of the chronicler's 'magic reel' in the last chapter of *The Old Curiosity Shop* suggests that he thought cinematically. Some see him as the forefather of the new medium: he translates so well to the screen because he is really writing for it. The ground-breaking Russian film director Sergei Eisenstein analysed *Oliver Twist* at length to show Dickens using cinematic techniques such as montage and dissolves. The novel is full of passages which look as if made for film, with Dickens creating a progression of images, rhythms, and sound.

Here, for example, is the sequence in which Oliver is chased by a crowd mistaking him for a thief:

> 'Stop thief! Stop thief!' There is a magic in the sound. The tradesman leaves his counter; and the carman his waggon; the butcher throws down his tray; the baker his basket; the milkman his pail; the errand-boy his parcels; the schoolboy his marbles; the paviour his pick-axe; the child his battledore. Away they run, pell-mell, helter-skelter, slap-dash: tearing, yelling, and screaming: knocking down the passengers as they turn the corners: rousing up the dogs, and astonishing the fowls; and streets, squares, and courts, re-echo with the sound.
>
> (Chapter 10)

If a favourite with many, *Oliver Twist* has had its share of controversy. In Dickens's day the problem was the glamorization of crime, and at least one dramatization was banned as harmful. In the twentieth century the depiction of Jews was the issue. Dickens himself toned down references to 'the Jew' in a later edition, in response to a Jewish reader who complained to him about his anti-semitism. One of the most famous adaptations, David Lean's 1948 film, led to rioting on the streets, with Jews in post-war Berlin protesting against the depiction of Fagin. The film was withdrawn from Berlin and banned for two years in the United States.

But Oliver was irresistible. Television adaptations and musicals joined film and theatre versions. They all include the scene of Oliver asking for more; it came to be a highlight, a sacred and defining event. In contrast, the powerful passages Dickens wrote of Fagin's trial and death cell are rarely dwelt on. Dickens takes us inside Fagin's consciousness; adaptations do not. The violent endings of Nancy and Bill Sikes are enough for us; we no longer have the stomach for Fagin's shocking last days. The musical *Oliver!*, whether on stage or film, is often people's introduction to Dickens. Its author, Lionel Bart, said he was inspired by a chocolate bar he loved called Oliver—the wrapper showed a boy asking for more.

At the end of the film version of *Oliver!* Fagin dances off into the sunset with the Artful Dodger: good adaptations have fertile lives of their own. New versions respond to the streets which inspired the novel. Twenty-first-century films update and deliver Oliver into underworlds of male prostitution and drugs. He relocates to New York, Toronto, Cape Town; he is sent to post-Soviet times in *Twistov*. On the page he is constantly reappearing—sixty-five new editions over the twenty years between 1984 and 2004. He has featured in graphic novels, in murder-mystery weekends, on statues and playing cards, on T-shirts and feeding-bowls for pets, in marketing and advertising campaigns. He has been a girl—*Olivia Twisted*—and at the mercy of vampires in *Oliver Twisted*. The words on the cover inevitably: 'Please, sir, I want some gore.'

From Dickens himself readers wanted more and he gave it, prodigiously. The huge sweep of his novels makes them as extensive as cities, as complex as labyrinths, and as comforting as firesides to sit beside. Over the eight hundred pages and, for his first readers, the eighteen months of serial publication, a Dickens novel builds a parallel world to run alongside our own, an ample and welcoming family to be part of our daily lives. Fourteen and a half novels altogether, each of them different and distinct from the others. Then there were the Christmas books and stories, the essays and journalism, the travel-writing and the public speeches. And as if all that were not enough, he left behind more than fourteen thousand letters (there were probably many more), attesting to what we should have grasped by now: the sheer pleasure Dickens took in putting pen to paper.

2

Public and Private

During the last Christmas of his life Dickens played a memory game with his family in which players passed on words or phrases and added one more. His son recalled his father making 'his own contribution, "Warren's Blacking, 30, Strand" . . . with an odd twinkle in his eye'. No one there had a clue what this meant to Dickens; he guarded the secrets of his childhood but let them out in his writing. His inherent contradictoriness impelled him towards self-display on the one hand and concealment on the other. He needed contact with his audience; he valued the 'personal affection' which he frequently characterized as existing between his readers and himself. He was, however, his daughter Katey told George Bernard Shaw, 'most extraordinarily reticent for a man who was supposed to be so full of frankness and geniality'. The showman tended his privacy fiercely; reasons for this can be traced back to his childhood.

Child of the Marshalsea

Dickens was born in Portsmouth in February 1812. His father was a clerk in the Naval Pay Office and earned a good salary, but it was never enough. Charles had a peripatetic childhood, moving to follow his father's employment. From Portsmouth the family (Charles had one older sister, one younger sister, and three younger brothers; two more siblings died young) moved to London, then to Chatham in Kent, and then back to London. They also changed lodgings as their fortunes fluctuated and they needed to evade creditors. Dickens had lived at nearly twenty different addresses before he established a home for himself as an independent twenty-two-year-old.

When Charles was just twelve the family hit rock bottom; his father was imprisoned for debt in the Marshalsea prison. Dickens himself described this period of his life in what has come to be known as the autobiographical fragment, written at some time in the 1840s. As was the custom then, Mrs Dickens and the younger children migrated into prison too. Charles's older sister Fanny was studying as a boarder and piano pupil at the Royal Academy of Music, but Charles had not been sent to school since the family had left Chatham two years earlier. Now he was expected to support himself. He visited the family in prison but boarded outside on his own in lodgings, for what was to be the most painful episode of his life. Through family connections he was found work at Warren's warehouse, where he pasted the labels on bottles of boot-blacking. Charles was small for his age and not strong—prone to attacks of 'spasm' in his side when stressed. He felt totally abandoned. 'No advice, no counsel, no encouragement, no consolation, no support, from anyone that I can call to mind, so help me God,' he wrote in his autobiographical fragment, for the eyes of his close friend

John Forster alone. This fragment would later form the second chapter of Forster's biography of Dickens.

'The deep remembrance of the sense I had of being utterly neglected and hopeless; of the shame I felt in my position': this was the trauma which shaped the whole of Dickens's imaginative life. He kept it secret, but there would be teasing references in his books to polish and bottles of boot-blacking. The hyacinths which blossom in old blacking bottles in *Nicholas Nickleby* connote the flourishing young author nicely. In 'Mrs Lirriper's Lodgings', a story from the last decade of his life, the hard-working servant Sophy is perennially smudged with blacking. She explains: 'I took a deal of black into me ma'am when I was a small child being much neglected and I think it must be, that it works out.'

The boy who showed young Charles 'the trick of using the string and tying the knot' of the blacking bottles, and who cared for him when he was ill by filling empty blacking-bottles with hot water and applying 'relays of them to my side, half the day' was called Bob Fagin. By the evening Charles had recovered, but Bob

> did not like the idea of my going home alone, and took me under his protection. I was too proud to let him know about the prison; and after making several efforts to get rid of him, to all of which Bob Fagin in his goodness was deaf, shook hands with him on the steps of a house near Southwark Bridge on the Surrey side, making believe that I lived there. As a finishing piece of reality in case of his looking back, I knocked at the door, I recollect, and asked, when the woman opened it, if that was Mr. Robert Fagin's house.

Giving kindly Bob Fagin's name to his first major villain suggests that Charles felt his self-worth under attack from these new associations. 'No words can express the secret agony of my soul as I sunk into this companionship,' he wrote. He had believed he was destined for better things, and the dashing of 'my early hopes of growing up to be a learned and distinguished man' was a wound for life.

> My whole nature was so penetrated with the grief and humiliation of such considerations, that even now, famous and caressed and happy, I often forget in my dreams that I have a dear wife and children; even that I am a man; and wander desolately back to that time of my life.

All this, he told Forster, 'made me what I am'.

The autobiographical fragment seems to have unlocked him: 'that time' of his life he shortly afterwards transferred to the childhood of the first of his two great first-person novels, *David Copperfield.* 'No one has written better about childhood,' George Orwell observes in his essay on Dickens. When Orwell read *David Copperfield* as a nine-year-old, 'the mental atmosphere of the opening chapters was so immediately intelligible to me that I vaguely imagined they had been written *by a child*'. Dickens's innovation was to double-track the perspectives of the child and the adult looking back. His prose can be fireworks and exuberance, but it can also attend to the quiet reflective inner voice, what the novelist Graham Greene praised as Dickens's 'secret prose, the sense of a mind speaking to itself with no one there to listen'.

The book and the writing of it is memory work for David—no wonder it was one of Freud's favourite books. How to understand myself is what the opening sentence, with its distinctive pausing uncertainty, tells us the novel will be about: 'Whether I shall turn out to be the hero of my own life, or whether that station will be held by anybody else, these pages must show.' Those anybody elses crowd forward to usurp the child, to exploit and hurt him. Abused by his step-father Mr Murdstone, David finds refuge as his creator had, in fiction and fantasy.

> My father had left in a little room up-stairs, to which I had access (for it adjoined my own) a small collection of books which nobody else in our house ever troubled. From that blessed little room, Roderick Random, Peregrine Pickle, Humphrey Clinker, Tom Jones, The Vicar of Wakefield, Don Quixote, Gil Blas, and Robinson Crusoe, came out, a glorious host, to keep me company. They kept alive my fancy, and my hope of something beyond that place and time,—they, and the Arabian Nights, and the Tales of the Genii.
>
> (Chapter 4)

The child's solitude and privileged access to his father's legacy, the contrast between confined space and 'glorious host', the characters' names which are all like David himself eponyms, and so precious that they must be painstakingly transcribed: all this intensifies the experience of that 'blessed little room', and the child 'reading as if for life'.

The other legacy from Dickens's father John was the loquacious and improvident Mr Micawber, with his famous words of wisdom for the child.

> 'My other piece of advice, Copperfield,' said Mr Micawber, 'you know. Annual income twenty pounds, annual expenditure nineteen nineteen six, result happiness. Annual income twenty pounds, annual expenditure twenty pounds ought and six, result misery. The blossom is blighted, the leaf is withered, the God of day goes down upon the dreary scene, and—and in short you are for ever floored. As I am!'
>
> To make his example the more impressive, Mr Micawber drank a glass of punch with an air of great enjoyment and satisfaction, and whistled the College Hornpipe.
>
> (Chapter 12)

A period of despair and searing shame for the young Charles, but with what panache he converts it to pleasure for both Micawber and reader.

Although John Dickens was soon at liberty thanks to an inheritance, his son would never quite release himself. Prisons abound in his writing. Three decades later he honoured jail-born Little Dorrit with the title 'Child of the Marshalsea'; her first name is Amy, a me. Following his own family's Marshalsea episode, the young Charles was kept working in the rat-infested warehouse, probably for about a year, until there was a family quarrel. The child was then withdrawn, and his father said he should go back to school. But, wrote Dickens later, 'I never afterwards forgot, I never shall forget, I never can forget, that my mother was warm for my being sent back' to the warehouse.

Schooldays did not last long. By Charles's fifteenth birthday times were hard again. Charles was the eldest son and had to earn his living, this time not as a factory boy but as a solicitor's clerk in Gray's Inn. A lowly position, it was at least a start in a professional environment, and Dickens could see his way upwards. Learning shorthand was the key. His maternal uncle John Barrow was a newspaper reporter and probably steered his nephew towards freelance court-reporting work. In 1831 Charles found steady employment as a parliamentary reporter on Barrow's new venture, *The Mirror of Parliament*, a weekly record of parliamentary proceedings. He also submitted small penny-a-line items to London newspapers, and—ever keen for self-improvement—obtained a ticket for the British Museum Reading Room as soon as he could. He was following his maxim of doing something, 'for the time being, as if there were nothing else to be done in the world—the only likely way I know of, of doing anything'.

This also went for his first love affair which 'excluded every other idea from my mind for four years'. His letters to Maria Beadnell feature him as the romantic lover laying his devotion at her feet and bewailing his fate when she seems to blow cold. 'I never have loved and I never can love any human creature breathing but yourself,' he addressed her with the ardour of a twenty-one-year-old. Not so optimistic about his prospects as he was, Maria's parents sent her to Paris, and when she returned her behaviour was cooler, or in Charles's melodramatic words, 'little more than so many displays of heartless indifference'.

The romance was over, but it left its mark. Writing to Maria years later, he attributed his habit of concealing his emotions—'even to my children, except when they are very young'—to the 'wasted tenderness of those hard years'. This was in 1855; he was in his forties, and Maria had written to him out of the blue. Despite her warning him that she was toothless, fat, old, and ugly, he contemplated rekindling the adolescent flames. He flattered her by saying she was in 'little bits' of Dora, the pretty young beloved of David Copperfield. What he did not tell her, after they had actually met, was that he was about to put her in his next novel, *Little Dorrit*.

> Flora, always tall, had grown to be very broad too, and short of breath; but that was not much. Flora, whom he had left a lily, had become a peony; but that was not much. Flora, who had seemed enchanting in all she said and thought, was diffuse and silly. That was much. Flora, who had been spoiled and artless long ago, was determined to be spoiled and artless now. That was a fatal blow.
>
> (Book I, Chapter 13)

Absolutely in earnest about his feelings, Dickens could savage them and the harmless Maria mercilessly.

By the time he was twenty he was earning enough to enjoy being a young man about town. The theatre was a great draw; he went almost every night. He adored acting, and now planned to take it up professionally. He wangled an audition at Covent Garden and rehearsed diligently; his sister Fanny 'was in the secret, and was to go with me to play the songs'. Another possible career. 'See how near I may have been to another sort of life,' he remarked to Forster. But he came down 'with a terrible bad cold' and had to miss the audition. And then he 'began to write' his sketches and stories of London streets and people.

Boz

Dickens was twenty-one when his first sketch appeared in December 1833. 'A Dinner at Poplar Walk' begins: 'Mr Augustus Minns was a bachelor, of about forty as he said—of about eight-and-forty as his friends said.' That very first sentence, with those disruptive 'friends' bursting in, has the stamp of Dickens all over it. Mr Minns is a clerk, one of the London types Dickens observed with what his friend William Macready called his 'clutching eye'. Neat, retiring, methodical Mr Minns sounds just what we might expect a clerk to be like, but before the end of the first paragraph his author has already gleefully undermined him:

> He was not unamiable, but he could, at any time, have viewed the execution of a dog, or the assassination of an infant, with the liveliest satisfaction.

To begin with, Dickens wrote unpaid. The thrill of seeing his work in the *Monthly Magazine* was more than enough. 'I walked down to Westminster Hall', he told Forster, 'and turned into it for half an hour, because my eyes were so dimmed with joy and pride that they could not bear the street, and were not fit to be seen there.' More sketches followed, and in August 1834 he first signed himself 'Boz'—a nickname he borrowed from his youngest brother Augustus. Now his life was opening out. He became a reporter on *The Morning Chronicle,* a reforming newspaper. He covered political rallies, fires, and first nights. He moved into lodgings of his own, which he invited his brother Fred to share with him. For all his habits of suppression he was a sociable person. Through *The Evening Chronicle* he met Catherine, the daughter of its editor George Hogarth. Their courtship was rapid. Dickens was eager to be married and they were soon engaged. His letters to her shower her with affectionate nicknames: Katie, Tatie, Mouse, dearest darling Pig, dearest Wig.

1836 was his golden year. *Sketches by Boz* was published in book form, and *Pickwick* took off. In April 1836 he and Catherine were married, and by November he felt confident enough as a writer to resign from *The Morning Chronicle.* In April 1837 the young family moved to 48 Doughty Street in Bloomsbury, now the Charles Dickens Museum, a spacious house still imbued with the atmosphere of youthful success.

They had been there barely a month before disaster struck. Catherine's younger sister, seventeen-year-old Mary, was staying with them, and Dickens took her and Catherine to see a farce he had written. On their return Mary was suddenly taken ill; she died in his arms the following afternoon. Dickens's grief was extreme. He wore her ring on his finger all his life. He kept her clothes, and in his thoughts they 'moulder[ed] away in their secret places'. He wanted to be buried next to her when he died. 'I solemnly believe that so perfect a creature never breathed. I knew her inmost heart, and her real worth and value. She had not a fault,' he told a close friend. Thus idealized, Mary cast a long shadow over his fictional young women. In the short term and for the only time in his life Dickens failed to meet his serial deadlines. There were no June instalments of either *Pickwick* or *Oliver.* But within two months of Mary's death there was also his first trip abroad—what sounds like a jolly jaunt to France and Belgium.

Public Figure

Before he was thirty Dickens was one of the most famous men in Britain, with public dinners held in his honour (see Figure 2). He embraced all of what he described to Forster as 'the enthoosemoosy', happily taking for himself the nickname 'The Inimitable', bestowed upon him by one of his old schoolmasters during the publication of *Pickwick Papers*. Requests for autographs were granted, for locks of hair gracefully refused. With the advent of photography his face became famous, he was greeted by strangers in the street, his hand shaken; he was feted when he travelled. Acknowledging the performance aspect of celebrity, Dickens dressed flamboyantly for the part, flashy waistcoats a speciality. As a young man he was rather a dandy; his friend and rival author William Thackeray rudely dubbed him a butterfly. Throughout his life Dickens's appearance was fair game for snobs who objected to his background and popularity with a mass audience. Benjamin Armstrong, a vicar from Norfolk who heard him read in 1859, recorded in his diary that he reminded him of a hairdresser. But for all the showmanship Dickens was primarily a writer, locked into a tight schedule of self-imposed multiple commitments. Foremost were the novels. He was writing until the day of his death, and left *Edwin Drood* unfinished (and to a whole industry of Drood-completers).

Dickens always published in serial form, which was not a medium he invented but one he took, experimented with, and made his own. On our shelves his books may now look bloated, forbidding, outmoded, but when they first saw

Figure 2 Dickens signs off this engraving of Daniel Maclise's 1839 portrait of him for the frontispiece of *Nicholas Nickleby*, as if writing personally to the reader and adding what he called the 'famous flourish' of his flamboyant signature.

Figure 3 The original monthly instalments of *Little Dorrit*, 1855–57. At the front and back of each number were pages of advertisements, sometimes with tie-ins to the novel.

daylight they were slim and attractive (see Figure 3). They made their initial appearance either in monthly parts of three or four chapters, or in shorter episodes in his weekly journals. Dickens's first writing career was as a journalist, and he thrived on the deadline mentality: hearing the yet-to-be-written next number of *David Copperfield* requested in the bookseller's shop or the printer's boy knocking at the door for copy. He enjoyed the newspaperman's culture of urgency, of contemporaneity with his readers. Serialization is the medium of immediate response, and he could write himself out of tight spots. When the real person on whom a character seemed to be based protested he could change tack, as he did with Miss Mowcher in *David Copperfield*, though 'with a very bad grace', he told a friend. Miss Mowcher, a 'pursy dwarf' chiropodist, rehabilitates from shady procuress in the eighth number to arrester of disguised villains in the last number. The obvious disadvantage, 'the impossibility of trying back', was outweighed by the creative pressure it imposed and the rapport with his readership which it fostered.

In tandem with this punishing regime was Dickens's career as a magazine editor, from his mid-twenties onwards with *Bentley's Miscellany*. From this post he kept threatening to resign, and did so after two years. A year later he started again with a new weekly journal, *Master Humphrey's Clock*, for which he was editor and sole contributor. In it he published two novels: *The Old Curiosity Shop* and *Barnaby Rudge*. His next experiment was travel, to America in 1842, where he was an instant success, mobbed wherever he went. 'People *eat* him here!' wrote one witness. He revelled in the spotlight until its rapid cut-off when he tried campaigning for the reform of international copyright—in those days authors earned nothing from work published abroad. At that point America and Dickens fell out of love with each other. 'This is not the Republic of my imagination,' he wrote to Macready; the sight of slavery in Virginia 'pained me very much'. Nevertheless he was able to capitalize on the trip in *American Notes*. This travel-writing was a new genre for him, and there was more experimentation the following year with *A Christmas Carol*, the invention of the Christmas book.

Meanwhile—that constant refrain in any account of Dickens's life—the children kept on coming: ten in sixteen years. It was cheaper to live abroad. During the 1840s he and his family decamped for long stays in Italy, Paris, and Switzerland. This led to more travel-writing with *Pictures from Italy*, but he had not lost his hankering for journalism. Taking on the editorship of the new radical newspaper *The Daily News* in 1846 was one of his few misjudgements, and he lasted only a few weeks. In Forster's verdict, 'nobody could be a worse [newspaper] editor than Dickens'. But he bounced back with new ideas for a periodical. In 1845 he saw its guiding presence as *The Cricket*, which was to disseminate 'Carol philosophy, cheerful views, sharp anatomization of humbug, jolly good temper'. Four years later it was the 'SHADOW, which may go into any place . . . and be supposed to be cognisant of everything'.

Finally, in 1850 he settled on *Household Words*—so called, he explained in its opening manifesto, because 'We aspire to live in the Household affections, and to be numbered among the Household thoughts, of our readers'. From then until his death in 1870 he edited it and its successor, *All the Year Round*—a weekly obligation for twenty years. He liked the steady income and sales, and the closeness to his audience. His editorial style was hands-on. He solicited fiction from leading authors: Elizabeth Gaskell was high on his list, and so was George Eliot, but she declined. He read all the unsolicited contributions and replied to their hopeful authors—sometimes rather caustically if he thought they had not tried hard enough. His own contributions were a mix of journalism, essays, and fiction. *Hard Times* was published in *Household Words*, and *A Tale of Two Cities* and *Great Expectations* in *All the Year Round*, which carried more fiction than its predecessor and did well with Wilkie Collins's masterpieces, *The Woman in White* and *The Moonstone*. Some of the journalism was pioneering: the 'process' articles, which were a species of industrial tourism, and the travel journalism which George Sala sent from St Petersburg after the Crimean War. As an editor Dickens was meticulous. 'Four hours of close attention', he reported to Forster from holiday in Boulogne in 1856, 'and the dreadful spectacle I have made of the proofs—which look like an inky fishing-net.' The overall tone was constantly monitored. 'Brighten it, brighten it, brighten it!' he urged his trusty sub-editor William Wills on being sent the proofs of a number which read, he complained, like 'stewed lead'.

His high public profile meant he was in demand as a speaker in support of good causes. This was something he excelled at, despite his dislike of what he called 'speechification'. Characters who indulge in it in his novels are self-important, uninterested in the welfare of others, and to be mistrusted, such as the Reverend Chadband in *Bleak House*, who sounded, says Jo the impoverished crossing-sweeper, 'as if he wos a speakin' to his-self, and not to me' (Chapter 47). Mr Honeythunder earns the newly-minted adverb 'platformally' for his pompous performances in *Edwin Drood* (Chapter 17). For his own speeches Dickens prepared assiduously so that he knew what he was talking about. He found out what was being taught at the new Mechanics Institutes for working men and women when he spoke on their behalf. At the General Theatrical Fund annual dinner he was a regular fixture. He stressed that the fund was not for the stars but the supporting cast—those 'poor actors who drink wine from goblets, in colour marvellously like toast and water' in ramshackle provincial theatres like the one he had visited 'the other night . . . where no particular piece belonged to the immense night in the bill, where generally people walked in and out, where a sailor fought a combat with anyone he chanced to meet and who happened to be in possession of a sword'.

He spoke at grand venues such as the Mansion House, but also in rooms above pubs for the benefit of small-scale causes, such as the Gardeners' Benevolent Institution. The gardeners pay in when they can and receive when they need; a miniature welfare state which Dickens approves of wholeheartedly. He pitches jokes appropriate to the occasion, describing the Gardeners' Institution as 'for the first years of its existence not particularly robust, and to have been placed in a shaded position, receiving somewhat more than its needful allowance of cold water'. He could be relied on by the community of print-workers, newspaper men, and newspaper sellers. I am still one of you, he tells the Newspaper Press Fund dinner in 1865, and 'have never forgotten the fascination of that old pursuit'. To much applause.

By the late 1840s he felt financially secure, despite the never-ending depredations from family members—his 'blood-petitioners' he called them bitterly. Now he could devote time to the issues of social reform which his novels were highlighting so successfully. The philanthropic heiress Angela Burdett Coutts was a good friend; Dickens worked with her and brought worthy cases to her attention. Education was a priority, for children and adults alike. He threw himself into causes he believed in, such as the

Guild of Literature and Art, which he and fellow novelist Edward Bulwer-Lytton created as a self-help hardship institution for artists and writers in the 1850s. They raised substantial amounts through their amateur dramatics (Queen Victoria attended a performance and donated handsomely). Aspiring to improve the status of authorship as a profession, Dickens laboured on even when the Guild ran into administrative sand.

His most sustained venture in social work was the home which he and Miss Coutts founded for young women coming from workhouses and prisons, and from the streets and slums of London. Urania Cottage in Shepherd's Bush had room for only thirteen inmates, which was much smaller than other asylums and refuges, because it was to be a 'home', an 'innocently cheerful Family' in Dickens's words. This was progressive thinking for its time. Dickens micromanaged the whole project, choosing the furniture and even selecting the material for the young women's clothes. They should not wear uniforms, he thought—too institutional—but have the bright colours that he himself enjoyed wearing. He interviewed staff and prospective inmates, and programmed every hour of every day, with a strict but liberal regime designed to train the young women to become good domestic servants. After about a year they should be ready to start new lives abroad. Miss Coutts paid their passage to the colonies. Dickens hoped they would marry, but Miss Coutts was less keen. Some of them did, and sent back enthusiastic letters. Commenting on one to Miss Coutts, Dickens enjoyed envisaging the three-dimensional happy endings: 'It is most encouraging and delightful! Imagining backward to what these women were and might have been, and forward to what their children may be.' For over a decade, from the mid-1840s to the mid-1850s, Dickens kept a vigilant eye on Urania Cottage. 'Active management' was how he described his role. He supervised the hiring and firing of staff, and got to know the inmates well. He interviewed them twice—once before they came to decide if they were suitable, and then when they had settled in he would take down their life-stories, which he forbade them to tell anyone else. These secret histories, affording him privileged glimpses into London's seamy underworld, he recorded in a Casebook, now lost. The traces of the young women's lives survive in the 1853 article he wrote about Urania Cottage for *Household Words*, 'Home for Homeless Women', and in all those foundlings and orphans, servants, laundresses, and child-carers, seamstresses and actresses, petty thieves and prostitutes, who swarm through his novels of the late 1840s and 1850s.

All this on top of his monthly novel deadlines and the weekly regime of the magazines: 'that great humming-top *Household Words*, which is always going round with the weeks and murmuring "Attend to me!"' as he described it to Leigh Hunt. Dickens thrived on having too much to do. The thousands of letters he wrote in the interstices of his other exertions—he reckoned he wrote 'at the least, a dozen a day'—are the nearest we have to his autobiography. They bring us up close to his packed life as writer, editor, and social campaigner, as well as giving us first-hand access to him as lover, husband, and father.

There was also his strenuous social life. Excess in the diary as well as on the page. The letters brim with invitations, acceptances, regretful refusals, arrangements for theatre trips and country excursions. Male friendships were important to him: John Forster from his earliest writing days, appointed biographer-in-waiting; the artists Clarkson Stanfield and Daniel Maclise; the actor William Macready; the novelist Wilkie Collins. He entertained lavishly. Elizabeth Gaskell enjoyed running jokes with him about the plain gold dinner service the Dickens family used on quiet days. Family birthdays were celebrated in style, especially those of his oldest son Charley, who had helpfully arrived on Twelfth Night, a popular day for parties. And he never forsook his passion for the theatre, marshalling friends for the amateur dramatics which he masterminded: choosing plays, distributing parts, cajoling cast members, directing rehearsals, ordering costumes and props, and taking the leading roles himself. Acting, which both conceals and reveals, suited him admirably. Organizing the theatricals was, he said, 'like writing a book in company'.

Restlessness

Dickens knew he was a driven man. He was a compulsive walker: four miles an hour, ten to fifteen miles by day or night. 'If I couldn't walk fast and far', he said, 'I should just explode and perish.' By his mid-forties he seems to have been heading for a crisis. 'Whatever it is, it is always driving me, and I cannot help it,' he told Forster in 1854, who diagnosed 'restlessness'. Dickens took on yet more commitments. Needing professional actresses to replace his daughters on a tour of his theatrical troupe to Manchester in 1857, he called on Frances Ternan and her daughters. The youngest, Ellen (Nelly), was eighteen, the age of Dickens's second daughter Katey. We do not know when Nelly and Dickens became lovers, but over the next few years Dickens's domestic life fell apart. Rewriting history, he told Miss Coutts that his marriage had been 'for years and years as miserable a one as ever was made', and that Catherine had never been a proper mother to her children—although well into the 1850s his letters to Catherine indicate warmth and a well-shared life. In 1858 he pushed her out of the family home, separating her from her children, the youngest of whom was only six.

'My father was like a madman when my mother left home', his daughter Katey told a friend much later; 'this whole affair brought out all that was worst—all that was weakest in him.' It was not enough for his marriage to fail; Dickens had to appear as the wronged party. He issued a Personal Statement—in effect a press release—which he thought would exonerate him to the world, although few readers could presumably understand it. It appeared in *The Times* and in Dickens's own magazine, *Household Words*. His good friend Mark Lemon refused to print it in *Punch*, and Dickens never spoke to him again.

It was not unusual for men in Dickens's circle to keep mistresses (the novelist Wilkie Collins and the artist William Frith both did), but Dickens's image as standard-bearer for family values put him in a difficult position. During the last twelve years of his life he strenuously pursued a divided life. For public Dickens this was a time of exposure and recognition. He had been giving readings for charity since the early 1850s, and in 1858 he went professional with an ambitious and gruelling programme of public readings. This was a new arena for his theatrical proclivities, and he exploited its potential remorselessly. For these one-man shows he adapted scenes from his novels, which he performed rather than read, startling audiences with his dramatic intensity. His tours criss-crossed England and took him to Scotland, Ireland, France, and America with nearly five hundred readings altogether.

The readings dominated his last years. Forster protested that they were demeaning, but Dickens welcomed both the personal contact with his readers and the money he needed to maintain himself, Catherine, and Nelly in separate houses. In 1856 he had become a proud house-owner for the first time, with the purchase of Gad's Hill Place in Kent—the house his father had encouraged him to work hard and dream of owning when he was a child. The most famous Victorian, he was granted an audience with the Queen in the last year of his life.

On the other hand, his was a life of secrets. 'A wonderful fact to reflect upon', he wrote at this time in *A Tale of Two Cities*, 'that every human creature is constituted to be that profound secret and mystery to every other' (Book I, Chapter 3), and he made sure that he was. In 1860 he made a huge bonfire and burnt all his correspondence. 'Would to God every letter I had ever written was on that pile,' he exclaimed. This was a time for cutting old ties. He broke with family and friends, quarrelled with the publishers of *Household Words*, left them, and started up a new magazine, *All the Year Round*. He gave up his London house and lived above the office—his 'gypsey tent', he called it. He supported Nelly in houses near London and spent time with her in France. According to information from Dickens's son Henry, passed on via a friend of his sister Katey, Nelly gave birth to a boy who died; but no evidence exists for this claim.

In his writing he continued to experiment. The Uncommercial Traveller essays in *All the Year Round* try a new kind of life writing, a quieter reflective voice. For all the indicators of racism which some modern critics detect in his later writings, Dickens could surprise himself and his readers with his leaps of tolerance. In his 1863 essay 'Bound for the Great Salt Lake' he boards a ship of migrating Mormons determined to mock them. He intends 'to bear testimony against them if they deserved it, as I fully believed they would', but finds 'to my great astonishment they did not deserve it'. The essay was admired by the philosopher Ludwig Wittgenstein for its open-mindedness. *Great Expectations*—the masterpiece from Dickens's last decade—was conceived as a twenty-part monthly, but when *All the Year Round*'s sales needed propping up Dickens instantly refashioned his story into a weekly serial for the magazine. Improvisation was again the spur. The novel returns to the first person of the child, this time in terror, shame, and guilt. Pip is burdened with secrets in the opening chapter; his progress is a tangle of aspiration, regret, and redemption.

Photographs from Dickens's last decade show him ageing too quickly. His health was adversely affected by a railway accident at Staplehurst, Kent, in 1865. Dickens was in the only carriage which did not go over the bridge crossing a small river, but hung, he told a friend a few days later, 'suspended and balanced in an apparently impossible manner'. Ten people were killed and another fourteen very badly injured. Unhurt but shaken, Dickens helped in 'getting out the dying and dead, which was most horrible', and in tending to the injured. He also 'instantly remembered' that he had left the manuscript of the latest number of *Our Mutual Friend* in the dangling carriage, and clambered back to retrieve it. The shock of the accident shadowed the rest of his life, and biographers often note that he died on its fifth anniversary.

Rejecting advice from friends and doctors, he embarked on long reading tours. His visit to America was a triumph, and he regained the acclaim he had forfeited on his visit twenty-five years earlier. But the programme there of more than seventy-five performances between December 1867 and April 1868 took its toll, as did the pressures of his secret life. He devised coded telegrams to let Nelly know whether it was safe for her to join him in America (he decided not), kept her in the shadows but named her as first legatee in his will. He said he wanted to die in harness—'Much better to die, doing'—and he did. He was half-way through *The Mystery of Edwin Drood*, a bold new departure featuring drugs and exotic oriental shenanigans, when he suffered a severe stroke. He died the next day.

3

Character and Plot

Characters are what Dickens is famous for. They crowd and flock through his novels—roughly two thousand named characters, and multitudes more unnamed. The original illustrations by George Cruikshank and Hablot K. Browne ('Phiz'), crammed with people, convey the sense of plenitude (see Figure 4). Many Dickens characters have achieved the fictional gold standard of life beyond the page, populating the empire of the collective imaginary. 'Dickens excelled in character,' wrote T. S. Eliot in his essay on Wilkie Collins and Dickens; 'in the creation of characters of greater intensity than human beings'. On the other hand, Dickens's characterization has been targeted for criticism, as have his plots. His characters are condemned as caricatures with no inner life, his plots as improbable and impossible to follow.

Names, Bodies, Clothes

Dickens seems to have started his characters from the outside and the label on the outside, with names. As with everything else, so with names: Dickens never just does one thing. Puns, jokes, onomatopoeia, metonymy, satire,

Figure 4 'The Emigrants', *David Copperfield*, Chapter 57, by Hablot K. Browne, Dickens's principal illustrator over many years. 'No other illustrator', wrote G. K. Chesterton, 'ever breathed the true Dickens atmosphere.'

suggestiveness from lightest to heaviest. Mr M'Choakumchild in *Hard Times* is the dry fact-obsessed schoolmaster, Wackford Squeers in *Nicholas Nickleby* the cruel one. Ebenezer Scrooge and Arthur Gride are misers, Sir Leicester Dedlock a representative of moribund aristocracy. The death bell already knells in Little Nell's name. 'Much deliberation' went into the choice, according to Forster, listing some of the surnames Dickens considered—Sweezleden, Sweezleback, Sweezlewag, Chuzzletoe, Chuzzleboy, Chubblewig, Chuzzlewig—before settling on Chuzzlewit. Dickens described his mind 'running, like a high sea, on names—not satisfied yet, though', as

Thomas Mag, David Mag, Wellbury, Flowerbury, Magbury, Copperboy, Topflower, and Copperstone all precede David Copperfield. Where the Chuzzlewit candidates are outrageous and comic, the Copperfield variants point to flowers, wells, things buried: the psychological terrain for a novel about memory. Dickens's names are at the eccentric end of the individuality spectrum, and individuality is the point. Names too similar to each other do not augur well. In *Bleak House* Lord Coodle, Sir Thomas Doodle, and the Duke of Foodle, Buffy, Cuffy, and Duffy all belong to the same stultifying political cabal, stuck together in rhyming impasse.

What Dickens likes best is riffing on his own name. In his letters he is Dick. 'On this day two and thirty years ago, the planet Dick appeared on the horizon' runs an invitation to one of his birthday parties. He cuts himself off in the middle of a long letter, 'as if there were no undone number, and no undone Dick!' His novels take his name to ring the changes on what might have been his fate. In *Oliver Twist* Dick is the weakly child Oliver leaves behind him at the baby-farm; Charley Bates is the Dodger's cheeky chum (punningly referred to as Master Bates), and the Dodger's surname Dawkins not so far away from Dickens. In *The Old Curiosity Shop* Dick Swiveller is a lively young legal clerk, while Charley in *Bleak House* is an orphaned thirteen-year old girl, labouring as a washerwoman to support her siblings. Less sympathetic is prentice-teacher Charley in *Our Mutual Friend*, not above exploiting his sister to get on in the world. Mr Dick in *David Copperfield* is a sort of holy fool obsessed by King Charles the First's head. Dickens was apparently 'much startled' when Forster pointed out the initials were 'but his own reversed' for David Copperfield. 'Why else, he said, should I so obstinately have kept to that name when once it turned up?'—in this novel mirroring his own experiences.

From names to bodies: the visual was crucial. All the novels apart from *Hard Times* and *Great Expectations* originally appeared with illustrations. Hablot K. Browne was Dickens's principal illustrator, but many others, some very distinguished, were also called upon: in the early years George Cruikshank, Robert Seymour, Robert Buss, and George Cattermole, and for the lavish Christmas books John Leech, Richard Doyle, John Tenniel, Daniel Maclise, Edwin Landseer, Clarkson Stanfield, and Frank Stone. Samuel Palmer provided the illustrations for *Pictures from Italy*, and for his last two novels Dickens turned to a younger generation of artists: Marcus Stone, Charles Collins, and Luke Fildes. Dickens liked to work closely with his illustrators, and was attentive to the minutest detail and gesture. 'Don't have Lord Decimus's hand put out,' he wrote to Browne about a very minor character in *Little Dorrit*; 'because that looks condescending; and I want him to be upright, stiff, unmixable with mere mortality.'

For Dickens, the body cannot choose but signal. The 'much flushed' magistrate Mr Fang in *Oliver Twist*, for example: 'If he were really not in the habit of drinking rather more than was exactly good for him, he might have brought an action against his countenance for libel, and have recovered heavy damages' (Chapter 11). Madame Defarge's strong features and 'darkly defined eyebrows' do not bode well in *A Tale of Two Cities* (Book I, Chapter 5). Nor do

Hortense's 'feline mouth and general uncomfortable tightness of face, rendering the jaws too eager and the skull too prominent' in *Bleak House* (Chapter 12). Mrs Plornish's introduction of her husband, plasterer and former bankrupt, to Arthur Clennam in *Little Dorrit* comes after a brief description: 'A smooth-cheeked, fresh-colored, sandy-whiskered man of thirty. Long in the legs, yielding at the knees, foolish in the face, flannel-jacketed, lime-whitened. "This is Plornish, sir."' (Book I, Chapter 12). After the check list which ranges from facial features to yielding knees and back to 'foolish in the face', Mrs Plornish's simple words act as summary and presentation to the reader: this is Plornish, we feel we know who Mr Plornish is. Faces can easily convey more than one message, such as the landlady Mrs Todgers in *Martin Chuzzlewit*, 'with affection beaming in one eye, and calculation shining out of the other' (Chapter 8). People who do not want to be read have to keep their faces averted, as do many young women who feel threatened. But readability is usually a sign of worth, and inscrutable characters like lawyer Tulkinghorn in *Bleak House* are not to be trusted.

Clothes, like faces, are the first thing we see on meeting someone, and they always set Dickens's imagination going. The early Boz sketch 'Meditations in Monmouth-street' celebrates the second-hand clothes for sale in the street which beget 'meditations', 'speculating', 'conjuring up', and 'revery'. The narrator fills the empty clothes with bodies so that they come to vigorous life:

> whole rows of coats have started from their pegs, and buttoned up, of their own accord, round the waists of imaginary wearers;

> lines of trousers have jumped down to meet them; waistcoats have almost burst with anxiety to put themselves on; and half an acre of shoes have suddenly found feet to fit them, and gone stumping down the street.

The clothes march through space and then time, with a consecutive narrative for some suits which Dickens decides all belonged to the same man at different periods. 'There was the man's whole life written as legibly on those clothes, as if we had his autobiography engrossed on parchment before us.' The story starts with the small sweet-eating child—'the numerous smears of some sticky substance about the pockets, and just below the chin'—and proceeds through message-lad's long-worn suit through 'smart but slovenly' man-about-town to end inevitably with prison garb and disgrace.

Dickens's characters can make their clothes speak forcibly. In *Great Expectations* the jilted Miss Havisham, still clad in the wedding dress she should have been married in years ago, is a famous example of statement clothes, while Pip's grudging sister also expresses herself sartorially. She 'almost always wore a coarse apron, fastened over her figure behind with two loops, and having a square impregnable bib in front, that was stuck full of pins and needles'. These sometimes get into the bread she cuts and subsequently 'into our mouths' (Chapter 2). When her husband, Joe the blacksmith, visits Pip newly 'gentle-folked'—'Joe considered a little before he discovered this word'—he insists on balancing his hat so precariously on the edge of Pip's mantel-piece that it keeps toppling off, being restored, toppling off again, an apt analogue for the relations between him and Pip at this point (Chapter 27). More agreeably, nautical

Captain Cuttle in *Dombey and Son* has such a large shirt collar 'that it looked like a small sail' (Chapter 4).

Some characters, the performers, deliberately use bodies, clothes, and names to send signals—practices swiftly seen through by the narrator's observing eye. Mr Mantalini ('originally Muntle'), the extravagantly dressed confidence trickster in *Nicholas Nickleby*, 'had whiskers and a moustache, both dyed black and gracefully curled.... He had married on his whiskers; upon which property he had previously subsisted, in a genteel manner, for some years; and which he had recently improved, after patient cultivation by the addition of a moustache, which promised to secure him an easy independence' (Chapter 10). Another fake, Mr Turveydrop in *Bleak House*, primps himself up elaborately in order to sponge off his good-natured son:

> He was a fat old gentleman with a false complexion, false teeth, false whiskers, and a wig.... He was pinched in, and swelled out, and got up, and strapped down, as much as he could possibly bear. He had such a neck-cloth on (puffing his very eyes out of their natural shape), and his chin and even his ears so sunk into it, that it seemed as though he must inevitably double up, if it were cast loose.... He had a cane, he had an eye-glass, he had a snuff-box, he had rings, he had wristbands, he had everything but any touch of nature; he was not like youth, he was not like age, he was like nothing in the world but a model of Deportment.
>
> (Chapter 14)

More appealing is the transparent dress-code devised by Sairey Gamp, layer-out of corpses in *Martin Chuzzlewit*:

> She wore a very rusty black gown, rather the worse for snuff, and a shawl and bonnet to correspond. In these dilapidated articles of dress she had, on principle, arrayed herself, time out of mind, on such occasions as the present; for they at once expressed a decent amount of veneration for the deceased, and invited the next of kin to present her with a fresher suit of weeds: an appeal so frequently successful, that the very fetch and ghost of Mrs. Gamp, bonnet and all, might be seen hanging up, any hour in the day, in at least a dozen of the second-hand clothes shops about Holborn.
>
> (Chapter 19)

People and Objects

'I think it is my infirmity to fancy or perceive relations in things which are not apparent generally,' Dickens wrote to Bulwer-Lytton in 1865. Even a standard thank-you letter can catch the infection. 'A thousand thanks for the noble turkey' ran one to Miss Coutts in 1841. 'I thought it was an infant, sent here by mistake, when it was brought in. It looked so like a fine baby.' The 'relations' between animate and inanimate, and the traffic between them, intrigued him. The Dickensian turn twists people into objects, objects into people, people into animals. He delights in connections and disconnections. Where, for instance, do bodies begin or end? How fitting that the earliest surviving letter from him as a thirteen-year-old schoolboy has a joke about a wooden leg—a lifelong source of amusement. Some years later, the gentleman at the Britannia Saloon advertised to dance the

Highland Fling 'his wooden leg highly ornamented with rosettes' was just the thing for an evening out with friends.

Bodies and bits, and bodies in bits: Dickens's eye takes a ghoulish snapshot of Mr Pecksniff in *Martin Chuzzlewit* eavesdropping in church, 'Looking like the small end of a guillotined man, with his chin on a level with the top of the pew' (Chapter 31). Mr Jingle in *Pickwick Papers* also relishes heads without bodies in his story prompted by the banal instruction to mind your head as the coach goes under a low archway. '"Terrible place—dangerous work—other day—five children—mother—tall lady, eating sandwiches—forgot the arch—crash—knock—children look round—mother's head off—sandwich in her hand—no mouth to put it in"' (Chapter 2). The boundaries of the body are not always where you expect. In *Hard Times* the dying Mrs Gradgrind, who has never been much more than a 'thin, white, pink-eyed bundle of shawls', is asked if she is in pain. '"I think there's a pain somewhere in the room", said Mrs Gradgrind, "but I couldn't positively say that I have got it."' (Book II, Chapter 9).

Dickens's use of synecdoche can distil character to one body-part. For the clerk Mr Wemmick in *Great Expectations* it is his 'post-office of a mouth' in which he pops pieces of biscuit as if posting them (Chapter 24). For villainous Uriah Heep in *David Copperfield* it is his clammy hands, obsequiously rubbed together. In *Little Dorrit*, trophy-wife Mrs Merdle is introduced as her bosom. 'It was not a bosom to repose upon, but it was a capital bosom to hang jewels upon.' Thereafter 'The bosom, moving in Society with the jewels displayed upon it' (Book I, Chapter 21) is how Mrs Merdle progresses majestically through the novel.

Blurring the boundaries between animate and inanimate sometimes looks like an urban tendency. Houses and streets are anthropomorphized, like the Six Jolly Fellowship Porters tavern in *Our Mutual Friend*, which leans lopsidedly over the river 'but seemed to have got into the condition of a faint-hearted diver who has paused so long on the brink that he will never go in at all' (Book I, Chapter 6), or the 'dowager old chimneys' which 'twirled their cowls and fluttered their smoke, rather as if they were bridling, and fanning themselves, and looking on in a state of airy surprise' (Book II, Chapter 5). Other streets can have the opposite effect. The mews behind the 'dismal grandeur' of the Dedlocks' mansion in *Bleak House* 'have a dry and massive appearance, as if they were reserved to stable the stone chargers of noble statues' (Chapter 48).

Dickens associates movement with life; for him it is in movement that we see the life-force in action. Much as he admired the Manchester Art Treasures Exhibition in 1857, he told his friend Macready, he thought people wanted 'more amusement, and particularly (as it strikes me) *something in motion*, though it were only a twisting fountain'. The owners of bodies which have got stuck are in trouble, like Miss Havisham in *Great Expectations* or Mrs Clennam in *Little Dorrit*. Bits of bodies which move when they should not can be comic, like Silas Wegg's wooden leg in *Our Mutual Friend*, elevating itself lewdly at the mention of buried treasure. One of the hallmarks of the *Household Words* house style was to imbue things with life, so that the commodities of Victorian consumer culture clamour for our attention with life-stories of their own.

Externalized Psychology

Dickens often gives us the inner by means of the outer. His psychology, wrote Viennese novelist Stefan Zweig, 'began with the visible; he gained his insight into character by observation of the exterior', his eye 'rendered acute by a superlative imagination'. Gesture and behaviour are freighted with meaning. Miss Tox snips and clips her pot plants 'with microscopic industry' as she learns that her hopes of becoming the second Mrs Dombey have come to nothing (Chapter 29). In *Hard Times*, Louisa Gradgrind, when kissed by the odious Mr Bounderby, rubs her cheek 'with her handkerchief, until it was burning red' (Book I, Chapter 6). The school-teacher Bradley Headstone in *Our Mutual Friend* acknowledges that he has finally been trapped in his gesture of slowly wiping his name out on the blackboard (Book IV, Chapter 15). Tiny moments can betray the inner man, like the 'sharp involuntary glance' which the starving Jingle 'cast at a small piece of raw loin of mutton' and told Mr Pickwick more of Jingle's 'reduced state than two hours' explanation could have done' (Chapter 42).

Possessions speak volumes. David Copperfield's step-aunt Miss Murdstone keeps her 'hard steel purse . . . in a very jail of a bag which hung upon her arm by heavy chains, and shut up like a bite' (Chapter 4). Mrs Pipchin, the 'ogress and child-queller' with whom young Paul Dombey boards, collects grotesque plants 'like hairy serpents; another specimen shooting out broad claws, like a green lobster; several creeping vegetables, possessed of sticky and adhesive leaves'

(Chapter 8). In *Bleak House*, the lawyer Mr Vholes shares his office with legal blue bags 'hastily stuffed, out of all regularity of form, as the larger sort of serpents are in their first gorged state' (Chapter 39).

'If he could give us their psychological character', wrote George Eliot of Dickens in 1856, 'their conceptions of life, and their emotions—with the same truth as their idiom and manner, his books would be the greatest contribution Art has ever made to the awakening of social sympathies.' But if there is little extended psychological analysis, there is, for example, an assured understanding of dependency culture in Uriah Heep—'"We was to be umble to this person, and umble to that... and abase ourselves before our betters"' (Chapter 39)—and its logical consequences. Unrealistic many of Dickens's eccentrics and grotesques may be, but their oddities can be the markers of internal damage and strain. And some of his characters do think deeply, their complex thought processes intricately traced by their author. Arthur Clennam in *Little Dorrit* suspects a guilty secret in his parents' past, and cannot handle the unwelcome thoughts which the suspicion might uncover.

> As though a criminal should be chained in a stationary boat on a deep clear river, condemned, whatever countless leagues of water flowed past him, always to see the body of the fellow creature he had drowned lying at the bottom, immovable, and unchangeable, except as the eddies made it broad or long, now expanding, now contracting its terrible lineaments; so Arthur, below the shifting current of transparent

> thoughts and fancies which were gone and succeeded by others as soon as come, saw, steady and dark, and not to be stirred from its place, the one subject that he endeavoured with all his might to rid himself of, and that he could not fly from.
>
> (Book II, Chapter 23)

Arthur condemned to the return of the repressed, long before Freud.

More submerged creatures haunt the depths in *Dombey and Son*, to give shape to young Florence Dombey's growing dread of her father's employee Mr Carker and 'the web he was gradually winding about her'. Beset by 'wonder and uneasiness' she deliberately tries to remember him more distinctly in order to reduce him 'to the level of a real personage', but it does not work. Is her antipathy to Carker something wrong with her, she thinks; could that something be to do with sex? That is something which the innocent Florence cannot know about, and Dickens reminds us she lacks the 'art and knowledge of the world' to deal with Carker. But she can have dread, and Dickens ends the passage with a brilliant image of Carker underwater, simultaneously inside and outside Florence:

> Thus, with no one to advise her—for she could advise with no one without seeming to complain against him—gentle Florence tossed on an uneasy sea of doubt and hope; and Mr Carker, like a scaly monster of the deep, swam down below, and kept his shining eye upon her.
>
> (Chapter 28)

Angels and Villains

Dickens's good characters are too good, his heroines are bland blanks: critics have complained that he cannot construct convincingly adult young women. He seems entranced by juvenile house-keeping. In *Martin Chuzzlewit*, Ruth Pinch makes a beef-steak pudding: 'Such a busy little woman', it was a 'perfect treat' for her brother Tom, and for us too Dickens implies,

> to see her with her brows knit, and her rosy lips pursed up, kneading away at the crust, rolling it out, cutting it up into strips, lining the basin with it, shaving it off fine round the rim; chopping up the steak into small pieces,

and so on and on through all the ingredients (except suet; reprimanded by a reader, Dickens added it in a subsequent number) to the predictably delicious result (Chapter 39).

While the saccharine is undeniable, it is worth saying that Dickens does give us complex female characters, often with elements of sexuality. Rosa Dartle in *David Copperfield*, Miss Wade in *Little Dorrit*, and Lady Dedlock in *Bleak House* all have back stories and a sexual history. Estella flushes with excitement in *Great Expectations* as she watches Pip and Herbert fight, and invites Pip to kiss her. Nancy in *Oliver Twist* lives on into our times as the tart with a heart, the victim of her pimp lover Bill Sikes. But Dickens gives her more inventiveness than that stereotype suggests. Forced by her lowlife companions into a plot to extricate Oliver from his middle-class patrons, she dresses up respectably with props provided by Fagin, and eventually takes to her role with zest:

> 'Oh, my brother! My poor, dear, sweet, innocent little brother!' exclaimed Nancy, bursting into tears, and wringing the little basket and the street-door key in an agony of distress. 'What has become of him! Where have they taken him to! Oh, do have pity, and tell me what's been done with the dear boy, gentlemen; do, gentlemen, if you please, gentlemen!'
>
> Having uttered these words in a most lamentable and heart-broken tone: to the immeasurable delight of her hearers: Miss Nancy paused, winked to the company, nodded smilingly round, and disappeared.
>
> (Chapter 13)

Dickens can never resist performance. In our enjoyment and admiration for Dodger and Nancy, and their swagger and verve, we overlook their designs on Oliver's innocent young soul.

The self-deprecating angel flitting through the fiction owes much to Mary Hogarth. Her first reincarnation as Rose Maylie in *Oliver Twist* sickens and nearly dies, but recovers. She reappears as Little Dorrit, as Agnes Wickfield in *David Copperfield,* and as Esther Summerson in *Bleak House.* Angels they may be, but they are also damaged and vulnerable. Rose feels the 'blight upon my name' of illegitimacy (Chapter 35). Agnes has an alcoholic father and is prey to Uriah Heep's sexual machinations. Little Dorrit is mercilessly exploited by her family. Esther is illegitimate, her self-esteem squashed by her punitive godmother. '"It would have been far better, little Esther,"' she tells her on her birthday, '"that you had had no birthday; that you had never been born!"' (Chapter 3).

Out of these potential victims Dickens fashions his heroine material. They can be surprisingly resourceful. Agnes runs a school to make ends meet; Esther is an efficient housekeeper; Little Dorrit finds training and employment for her elder siblings and herself. This competence combines with the magical ability to walk the streets of London undefiled, to face danger and be unharmed. Realism is fused with allegory, romance, religious parable: Dickens never does just one thing. In *Dombey and Son*, little Florence is lost on the streets of London and is rescued by gallant Walter Gay, who replaces her shoe 'as the prince in the story might have fitted Cinderella's slipper on' (Chapter 6). Fairy-tale in Thames-street, imaginary characters in the real docks of London.

On the other hand, Dickens's villains have had a good press. His fascination with the criminal and the pathological has long been recognized. Dostoevsky was one of the first novelists to take the lead from Dickens, and in our own culture the fascination shows no sign of abating. Dickens revels in putting us inside Fagin during his trial and beside him in the condemned cell. Violent Bill Sikes starts as a growling thug seen from the outside; but having murdered Nancy his guilt endows him with interiority, and Dickens devotes a whole chapter to 'The Flight of Sikes'. In slow motion and close focus he tracks his every move. The terror is in the detail, as Sikes tries to remove the evidence—'there were spots that would not be removed, but he cut the pieces out, and burnt them'—and escape from the horrifying apparition of the murdered woman. But it pursues him from London, 'that morning's ghastly figure following at his heels...its garments rustling in the leaves', and the thug disintegrates before our eyes. Then, in an extraordinary scene, he comes across some burning buildings and galvanizes into life. 'Hither and thither he dived that night: now working at the pumps, and now hurrying through the smoke and flame, but never ceasing to engage himself wherever noise and men were thickest...in every part of that great fire was he; but he bore a charmed life' (Chapter 48).

Those fires inside himself which he cannot put out: the mania of guilt engages Dickens more than the morality. The little room into which Jonas Chuzzlewit locks himself before and after he commits murder is 'a blotched, stained, mouldering room, like a vault; and there were water-pipes running through it, which at unexpected times in the night, when other things were quiet, clicked and gurgled suddenly, as if they were choking'. It is this squeezed gothic kennel rather than the scene of his crime which frightens Jonas; 'his hideous secret was shut up in the room, and all its terrors were there' (Chapter 47).

When angels and villains meet, Dickens favours non-realism. *The Old Curiosity Shop* has one of his most egregious villains and one of his most angelic heroines. Little Nell has been the best-loved and most mocked character in English literature. Readers in New York are reported to have lined the quaysides agog for the next instalment arriving from London, shouting 'Is Little Nell still alive?' Her death came to be the classic type of Victorian sentimentality, and was thus soon reviled. Oscar Wilde's view was that one would need a heart of stone to read the death of little Nell without laughing. The critic John Ruskin accused Dickens of killing her for the market as a butcher kills a lamb, but although Dickens knew it was good for business he was nevertheless sincere and counted himself among the weepers. 'Dear Mary' dies again, he told Forster as he put the finishing touches to the novel—'such a very painful thing to me'; on the other hand he was also out partying till after five in the morning.

Although Nell is more active—and laughs more—than her critics may remember, on one level they are right. She staggers under the weight of being an emblem of purity. The first scene introduces her to us as a child in a fairy-tale, making her solitary way through the streets of night-time London. Later, leading her aged grandfather away from danger, she is evoked through archaic language and the novel's many references to *The Pilgrim's Progress* and Shakespeare.

In symmetrical opposition to this allegory of goodness is the dwarfish Daniel Quilp. Pantomime villain and comic monster, he pops up 'like an evil spirit' when least expected. He terrorizes Nell, pursuing her even to her bedroom, where he bounces on her bed. Kissing her lasciviously—'"What a nice kiss that was—just upon the rosy part"'—he invites her to be '"my number two"' (Chapter 6). His energy and appetite are demonic: 'he ate hard eggs, shell and all, devoured gigantic prawns with the heads and tails on, chewed tobacco and water-cresses at the same time and with extraordinary greediness.' (Chapter 5). '"I hate your virtuous people!"' he crows as he downs pints of boiling rum (Chapter 48); and '"Where I hate, I bite"' (Chapter 67). Quilp is 'a perpetual nightmare to the child' (Chapter 29), but more terrifying still is the threat from within. 'Immeasurably worse, and far more dreadful' than Punch-like Quilp is her own grandfather. By day a 'harmless fond old man' (Lear set against Quilp's Richard III), by night he is a compulsive gambler, the horrible unnameable 'dark form' creeping into Nell's bedroom, invading her bed in search of money, 'groping its way with noiseless hands . . . the breath so near her pillow, that she shrunk back into it, lest those wandering hands should light upon her face' (Chapter 30).

This early novel represents Dickens's modes of characterization at their most extreme and expressive. But if the later novels are more realistic they draw upon the same cast of monsters and the same clashes between good and evil. The father who exploits his daughter reappears in William Dorrit trying to persuade his daughter Amy to look kindly on the jailer's son in order that life will be easier in prison for him. And running throughout the novels from first to last is the Dickens signature of superfluity—that super-abundance of characters on the periphery who may appear once or who never speak: right up to the boatman Lobley in the last number of the unfinished *Edwin Drood*, who 'danced the tight rope the whole length of the boat' just for the pleasure of it.

Improbable Plots

Dickens was sensitive to charges that his plots were far-fetched and implausible. His Postscript to *Our Mutual Friend* tackles head-on the 'odd disposition in this country to dispute as improbable in fiction, what are the commonest experiences in fact'. His customary defence is to cite evidence from current events that such things are so. In his Preface to *Bleak House* he claims that his treatment of the Court of Chancery is 'substantially true, and within the truth'. He likes to cite authorities: *The Lancet* medical journal for his portrayal of the Poor Law in *Our Mutual Friend*, and a parade of abstruse historians for the outrageous spontaneous combustion plot-line in *Bleak House*.

Dickens was being disingenuous. What critics mainly objected to are the tortuous wills unravelled in the last chapter, the fortuitous arrivals of long-lost relations. In his book on Dickens, admirer though he was, George Gissing felt compelled to 'speak of the sin, most gross, most palpable, which Dickens everywhere commits in his abuse of coincidence'. Dickens himself did not see it as abuse. 'On the coincidences, resemblances and surprises of life', wrote Forster in his biography, 'Dickens liked especially to dwell, and few things moved his fancy so pleasantly. The world, he would say, was so much smaller than we thought it; we were all so connected by fate without knowing it.'

Benevolent fate seems to be at work when Nicholas Nickleby meets his future benefactor in the street. Here is fortune smiling at last on the struggling young hero. Nicholas and Mr Cheeryble could easily have met inside the employment agency they are standing outside; after all, one of them is looking for employment and the other has a vacancy. But see how providential it is, Dickens's coincidence plot seems to be saying, that good employers and good employees should bump into each other on the street.

The chance meetings of *Bleak House* show a much less kindly fate at work. Here the 'connexion' between the rich and poor characters is central to the plot and is foregrounded as an explicit issue. 'What connexion', the narrator asks, 'can there have been between many people in the innumerable histories of this world, who, from opposite sides of great gulfs, have, nevertheless, been very curiously brought together!' (Chapter 16). The answer is provided by the plot, which puts Dickens's social and moral preoccupations into action.

Dickens also needs plot for suspense, that third ingredient of the tripartite imperative of Victorian popular fiction—'Make 'em laugh, make 'em cry, make 'em wait!'—which he structured into his method of publication from the start. Serial form builds waiting and suspense into the meaning of the novel and makes them a crucial part of the reading experience, which is why this book has tried to eschew plot spoilers. In Chapter 49 of *David Copperfield*, 'I am Involved in Mystery', Mr Micawber promises to tell David his '"inviolable secret"' about Uriah Heep '"this day week"'; the original readers would have to wait a month. Readers had to wait a week to learn the identity of the man lunging through the bushes at pretty Dolly Varden at the end of Chapter 20 of *Barnaby Rudge*, as they would to find out the import of the last words of Chapter 44 of *Great Expectations*, Mr Wemmick's terse note to Pip, 'DON'T GO HOME'. While such cliff-hangers are not as common as Dickens's reputation for them suggests, he does expect his readers to be able to wait and to remember, across long time-spans and with little prompting. The first readers of *Our Mutual Friend* heard of two characters called Jacob Kibble and Job Potterson in the first number in May 1864, then no more about them until

January 1865, and then nothing again until November. The first part of *Little Dorrit* ends with a reference to an iron box which does not reappear until the last number a year and a half later. Kibble, Potterson, and the iron box are all plot-functional, planted and held in readiness by the forward-thinking author.

As with character so with form, Dickens enjoys the mash-up of genre. He mixes up stark realism, broad satire, romance, fable, fairy-tale, farce, and tragedy, playing them against each other. Early in his career he chose a telling analogy for his methodology. 'It is the custom on the stage', he says in *Oliver Twist*, 'in all good, murderous melo-dramas: to present the tragic and the comic scenes, in as regular alternation, as the layers of red and white in a side of streaky, well-cured bacon' (Chapter 17). One moment the hero is 'weighed down by fetters and misfortunes', the next we are enjoying a comic song. Juxtaposition is all. These 'sudden shiftings of the scene' are justified, he says, 'from well-spread boards to death-beds', because such 'transitions' happen 'in real life' too. That was his defence, but more interesting is his appeal to melodrama, that exaggerated, expressive, moral, and above all popular cultural form.

To begin with improvisation was the spur, and the novels of the 1830s and early 1840s can seem as if they might sprawl indefinitely, with weak and implausible plot lines. They look back to the picaresque novels of Smollett and Fielding, the historical novels of Walter Scott. With *Dombey and Son* (1846–48) came a decisive change. From then on the novels would be more carefully planned, and Dickens kept working notes and memorandums (see Figure 5). 'I work

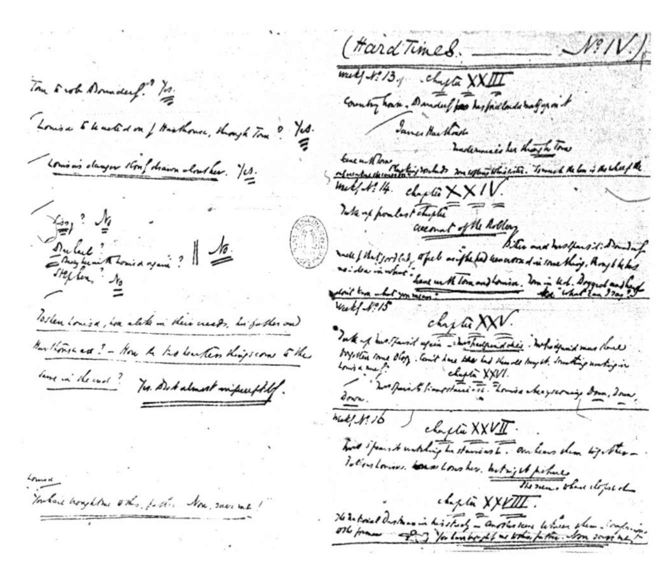

Figure 5 Manuscript of Dickens's working notes for *Hard Times*: left-hand side for planning and progress so far, right-hand side for division of content into chapters, as well as weekly and monthly parts.

slowly and with great care, and never give way to my invention recklessly, but constantly restrain it,' he told Bulwer-Lytton in 1865.

He wanted it every which way: the excitements of protracted publication, with his readers bound to him and living with his characters for a year and a half at a time; but he also wanted to draw his readers' attention to what in the Preface to *Little Dorrit* he called the merits of the whole.

'As it is not unreasonable to suppose that I may have held its various threads with a more continuous attention than any one else can have given to them during its desultory publication, it is not unreasonable to ask that the weaving may be looked at in its completed state, and with the pattern finished.' The Postscript to *Our Mutual Friend* again refers to the 'whole pattern which is always before the eyes of the story-weaver at his loom'. Both Preface and Postscript were written after their final monthly parts—thumping double numbers to reinforce the triumphant closure so long deferred that it deserves emphatic resolution, however forced and unlikely. That is the point of plot for Dickens: to link and connect, so that the lost and the random and the disparate will be brought together and given meaning, their places finally revealed in the 'whole pattern' of the universe of the book.

4

City Laureate

Dickens is our first and best novelist of the city. London in the mid-nineteenth century was the supreme modern urban space, and Dickens its chronicler. Acclaimed by his contemporary, the political commentator Walter Bagehot, as London's 'special correspondent for posterity', Dickens took the city for his first subject, and was instantly recognized for his skill in skewering what everyone had seen but nobody else had consciously noted. The first to celebrate the experiences of metropolitan living, he was also first to explore its horrors. He had, in the words of a character in *Pickwick Papers*, 'the key of the street' (Chapter 46). With his novels or journalism in your hand you had—and still have—a street guide. You know which real streets his characters are walking down. But while Dickens's London gazetteers steer us literally, Dickens also achieves something more. Articulating the city to itself, he shows us how to read it, how to live it. According to the novelist George Gissing, he 'taught people a certain way of regarding the huge city'. Dickens's London is at the same time literal and transformed: a hyperreal London. In his Preface to *Bleak House* he writes of dwelling 'upon the romantic side of familiar things'—and familiar places too we might add. It is not that the 'romantic' runs alongside the real, in the manner of magic realism, but rather that the real becomes invested with magic, irradiated and allegorized. Further, Dickens's predilection for extremes and oppositional modes of thinking flourishes in—perhaps had its genesis in—this environment where, as he writes in *Nicholas Nickleby*, 'there was a christening party at the largest coffin-maker's', where 'life and death went hand in hand; wealth and poverty stood side by side; repletion and starvation laid them down together' (Chapter 32). London is both goal to be aspired to and abyss to drag you down, source of energy and source of death, Jerusalem and inferno.

Muse

'Most of all', Forster writes about Dickens's childhood impressions of London, 'he had a profound attraction of repulsion to St. Giles's.' This was a slum area, and Dickens's response to it could well stand for his lifelong relationship to the whole city. His pavement-level perspective originated in his early solitary walks. As Tony Weller says of his son Sam in *Pickwick Papers*, '"I took a good deal o' pains with his eddication, Sir; let him run in the streets when he was wery young, and shift for his-self. It's the only way to make a boy sharp, Sir"' (Chapter 20). Tony Weller is a cab-driver, one of Dickens's urban heroes. His 'knowledge of London was extensive and peculiar' and reaches to the micro-level of the best spot in the pub: '"Take the box as stands in the first fire-place, 'cos there an't no leg in the middle o' the table, vhich all the others has, and it's wery inconwenient"' (Chapter 20). It was in London that Dickens's genius found its shape. 'I fitted my old books to my altered life', he recalled through the mouthpiece of David Copperfield, 'and made stories for myself, out of the streets, and out of men and women' (Chapter 11). Living in Switzerland in 1846, he acknowledged just how much he depended on the crowded streets of London, lamenting to Forster 'the absence of streets and numbers of figures'.

> I can't express how much I want these. It seems as if they supplied something to my brain, which it cannot bear, when busy, to lose. For a week or a fortnight I can write prodigiously in a retired place (as at Broadstairs), and a day in London sets me up again and starts me. But the toil and labour of writing, day after day, without that magic lantern, is IMMENSE!!

Those streets had launched Dickens as Boz the 'speculative pedestrian', speculating and investing in his own habitat. What Boz realizes so percipiently—for himself and for us—is the streets not as backdrop but as the makers of the drama. In two early linked sketches, 'The Streets—Morning' and 'The Streets—Night', Boz defamiliarizes and records the choreography of public urban living. Starting before dawn in the 'air of cold, solitary desolation', and much like the 'rakish-looking cat' stealthily crossing the road, Boz attends vigilantly to the first signs of movement and the next hour's building 'bustle and animation'. Ethnologist, anthropologist, and dramatist, Boz records the animal, vegetable, and edible contents of Covent Garden with equal gusto:

> The pavement is already strewed with decayed cabbage leaves, broken hay bands, and all the indescribable litter of

> a vegetable market: men are shouting, carts backing, horses neighing, boys fighting, basket-women talking, piemen expatiating on the excellence of their pastry, and donkeys braying.

Now he has us with him in the continuous present of the street, Boz can perform stunning shifts of pace and viewpoint. Skidding to a halt, he picks up the slow rhythm of the lazy apprentice 'who pauses every other minute from his task of sweeping out the shop and watering the pavement in front of it, to tell another apprentice similarly employed, how hot it will be today'; then he dives down the apprentice's perspective to watch the fast coach departing and follow it down into the country and his own memories, 'the green pond he was caned for presuming to fall into, and other schoolboy associations'.

For 1830s consumer Boz, the flaneur walking 'without any definite object', London offers itself as its amusements: Greenwich Fair, Vauxhall Gardens and Astley's circus, river trips, and private theatricals. For Boz, the draw is both the horses in the ring and the family watching, 'pa and ma, and nine or ten children', ranging from the baby 'in a braided frock and high state of astonishment' to fourteen-year-old George 'evidently trying to look as if he did not belong to the family'. And he also shows the other side of the coin. Gin-shops, pawnbrokers' shops, slums, Newgate prison. Boz shares his author's 'attraction of repulsion'. If the gin-shops start by being 'amusing'—Boz's favourite commendation—they end in drunkenness, 'riot and confusion'. Flaneurial detachment is abandoned in order to drive home the moral: 'Gin drinking is a great vice in England, but wretchedness and dirt are a greater; and until you improve the homes of the poor, or persuade a half famished wretch not to seek relief in the temporary oblivion of his own misery . . . gin-shops will increase in number and splendour.'

Dickens saw himself as the presiding spirit of the city. Master Humphrey, the elderly invalid persona adopted by the youthful Dickens to edit his new weekly magazine *Master Humphrey's Clock* in 1840, is a city walker. He opens *The Old Curiosity Shop* with the words 'Night is generally my time for walking' and a meditation on the sounds of city walking, 'that constant pacing to and fro, that never-ending restlessness'. Nine years later and about to start a new magazine (Master Humphrey did not last long), Dickens outlined his idea to Forster for its editorial persona as the 'SHADOW, which may go into any place . . . to loom as a fanciful thing all over London . . . a kind of semi-omniscient, omnipresent, intangible creature' at loose in the city—much like his own presence. In presenting the city to itself Dickens was in the vanguard of a trend. *The Illustrated London News* started in 1842. The new technology of photography had London as its centre and its subject. London was becoming more self-consciously visual; Dickens helped it to be so.

By the 1850s Dickens was wearying of London—'a vile place' he told Bulwer-Lytton in 1851—but his journalism continued to come from its heart. 'Night Walks', an essay from 1860, concentrates his lifelong addiction to urban night-walking into a virtuoso account of one night between midnight and dawn. Here we can see how the nocturnal city works for Dickens, refracted through the narrating persona he calls 'Houselessness'. Dickens can shed himself, be someone else as he moves through London. Other cities engaged him too. Paris, 'the most extraordinary place in the world', to be read as an 'enormous book', charmed him from his first visit in 1844. He got to know it intimately, once describing himself 'in a state of continual oscillation between London and Paris', and signing off a letter to Forster 'Charles Dickens, Français naturalisé, et Citoyen de Paris'. Every city has its own flavour for him; Marseilles is 'a fact to be strongly smelt and tasted' at the beginning of *Little Dorrit*. But London was the main attraction. Towards the end of his life he boasted that he knew it 'better than any one other man of all its millions'; and he probably did, with his sense of the specificity of every street and square, but at the same time that holistic apprehension expressed in *Bleak House* of the 'distant ringing hum, as if the city were a vast glass, vibrating' (Chapter 48).

Coming to the City

The young man coming to the city to seek his fortune is an old story. Dickens told it himself many times, with its stages of initiation, familiarization, taint, and survival. After all, he was himself a migrant to the city at the age of ten, and he situated many of his novels in this period of the 1820s, when the city first imprinted itself on his mind. Like David Copperfield at the same age, his impressions were filtered through the lens of the bookish child:

> What an amazing place London was to me when I saw it in the distance, and how I believed all the adventures of my

> favourite heroes to be constantly enacting and re-enacting there . . . I vaguely made it out in my own mind to be fuller of wonders and wickedness than all the cities of the earth.
>
> (Chapter 5)

City of extremes, and always the magnet. Living in the northern suburbs, Harriet Carker in *Dombey and Son* looks 'with compassion' on the weary 'stragglers' on their way to London.

> Swallowed up in one phase or other of its immensity, towards which they seemed impelled by a desperate fascination, they never returned. Food for the hospitals, the churchyards, the prisons, the river, fever, madness, vice, and death,—they passed on to the monster roaring in the distance, and were lost.
>
> (Chapter 33)

To Harriet's sad fancy the crowd goes one way, towards the devouring 'monster'. But Dickens can also describe the two-way in-and-out of commuting—a new phenomenon observed by Boz in 'Omnibuses' and 'The Streets—Morning'. Crowds surge through the Dickens city, a place of constant movement and change, above all the maker and marker of modernity. He can be brisk about nostalgia for the past, and his handling of the railway illustrates this well.

Dombey and Son is Dickens's novel of the railway, which is introduced as a force of nature erupting in the northern suburb of Camden Town: 'The first shock of a great earthquake had, just at that period, rent the whole neighbourhood to its centre.' Sentence structure is shaken and strained to convey the fractured landscape: 'Houses were knocked down; streets broken through and stopped; deep pits and trenches dug in the ground; enormous heaps of earth and clay thrown up; buildings that were undermined and shaking, propped by great beams of wood.' With zigzagging energy Dickens catches the details of the massive construction site:

> Here, a chaos of carts, overthrown and jumbled together, lay topsy-turvy at the bottom of a steep unnatural hill; there, confused treasures of iron soaked and rusted in something that had accidentally become a pond. Everywhere were bridges that led nowhere; thoroughfares that were wholly impassable.

Crashing his paragraph to a standstill in the 'mounds of ashes [which] blocked up rights of way, and wholly changed the law and custom of the neighbourhood', Dickens now suddenly switches direction from destruction to creation, with a sharp new paragraph: 'In short, the yet unfinished and unopened Railroad was in progress; and, from the very core of all this dire disorder, trailed smoothly away, upon its mighty course of civilisation and improvement' (Chapter 6).

Whether this is ironical or not is nicely balanced at this point, when the neighbourhood is still 'shy to own the Railroad'. But fast-forward nine chapters and a few years, and 'Bridges that had led to nothing, led to villas, gardens, churches, healthy public walks'. Landscape and railway move in unison: 'The carcasses of houses, and beginnings of new thoroughfares, had started off upon the line at steam's own speed, and shot away into the country in a monster train.' Now all is railway:

> railway hotels, coffee-houses, lodging-houses, boarding-houses; railway plans, maps, views, wrappers, bottles,

> sandwich-boxes, and time tables; railway hackney-coach and cab-stands; railway omnibuses, railway streets and buildings, railway hangers-on and parasites, and flatterers out of all calculation. There was even railway time observed in clocks, as if the sun itself had given in.
>
> (Chapter 15)

Progress, or death by materialism? Dickens's prose pulses between the two, with the kinetic dynamism that sustains it all:

> To and from the heart of this great change, all day and night, throbbing currents rushed and returned incessantly like its life's blood. Crowds of people and mountains of goods, departing and arriving scores upon scores of times in every four-and-twenty hours, produced a fermentation in the place that was always in action.

How could Dickens not love it; the 'very houses seemed disposed to pack up and take trips'.

Over the course of his novels, the young man coming to the city experiences more and more in the way of disaffection and failure. Newly arrived in London, *Martin Chuzzlewit*'s innocent Tom Pinch is comically 'quite disappointed to find, after half an hour's walking, that he hadn't had his pocket picked' (Chapter 36). A few years later, in *David Copperfield*, Dickens shaped his own childhood into a story of survival and success. He looks back on himself as the hungry child fending for himself, recalling the allure of stale pastry and stout pale pudding. Older and with money in his pocket, David throws himself into the pleasures of London life. The chapter 'My First Dissipation' is rite of passage recollected as comic disaster.

Going to the theatre drunk, he bumps into the much-admired Agnes. '"Agnes!" I said, thickly, "Lorblessmer! Agnes!... I'mafraidyou'renorwell"' (Chapter 24).

A decade later, *Great Expectations* gives a sadder account of the city. The expectations of the novel's title start to crumble as soon as Pip arrives in London and finds not the glory he was anticipating but something uglier and dirtier, and so impenetrable that he must take a cab when he does not need one because he cannot find his own way. Reaching the lawyer's office, he is 'oppressed by the hot exhausted air, and by the dust and grit that lay thick on everything', and escapes outside. 'So, I came into Smithfield [the cattle-market]; and the shameful place, being all asmear with filth and fat and blood and foam, seemed to stick to me' (Chapter 20). The cheek-by-jowlness of London continually dismays him. He feels 'contaminated' on his way to meet his beloved Estella after a prison tour with Wemmick, regretting that he has 'Newgate in my breath and on my clothes' (Chapter 32). He also has his man-about-town diversions, and joins a club called the 'Finches of the Grove: the object of which institution I have never divined, if it were not that the members should dine expensively once a fortnight, to quarrel among themselves as much as possible after dinner, and to cause six waiters to get drunk on the stairs'. Disillusion sets in.

> We were always more or less miserable, and most of our acquaintance were in the same condition. There was a gay fiction among us that we were constantly enjoying ourselves, and a skeleton truth that we never did.
>
> (Chapter 34)

City Life

The Dickens city grows its streets, buildings, people, and ways of living. Economics and class determine its contours. In this pre-Darwinian model of social evolution the city spawns those needed to sustain it: the burgeoning bureaucracy of clerks and lawyers, the shopkeepers and all the niche workers catalogued by Henry Mayhew in his *London Labour and the London Poor.* The city can be punishing, and its victims are often women, such as the two sisters Boz watches boarding 'The Prisoners' Van'. The elder girl, who 'could not be more than sixteen', banters with the crowd while her thirteen-year-old sister hides her face in shame. Boz reads them in sequence: 'What the younger girl was then, the elder had been once; and what the elder then was, the younger must soon become.' But if London is a graphic novel of downwardness and fall it is also one of survival, of dodging and diving. Impecunious lawyer's clerk Dick Swiveller in *The Old Curiosity Shop* enjoys the challenge of debt-evasion.

> 'I enter in this little book the names of the streets that I can't go down while the shops are open. This dinner to-day closes Long Acre. I bought a pair of boots in Great Queen Street last week, and made that no thoroughfare too. There's only one avenue to the Strand left open now, and I shall have to stop up that to-night with a pair of gloves.'
>
> (Chapter 8)

Twenty-five years and nine novels later, Dick's optimism has abated. *Our Mutual Friend* is, unusually for Dickens, set in the present, a 'dark greasy' city of dirt and waste. So much so that T. S. Eliot considered using a quotation from the novel—'He do the police in different voices'—as his title for *The Waste Land*. But for Dickens waste is not the end. Characters make their livings by feeding off and recycling the detritus of the city. North London is now not railway and civilization but giant dust heaps, a source of wealth continually poked at and scavenged to yield more. Even the dirty water in which gold and silver workers have washed their hands is bought by refiners. In Limehouse Hole—what a name—Pleasant Riderhood runs something called a Leaving Shop, unlicensed and at the bottom of the hierarchy of pawnshops. Dickens shows us the primitive squalor of the 'wretched little shop . . . little better than a cellar or cave' and itemizes its stock: 'a few valueless watches and compasses, a jar of tobacco and two crossed pipes, a bottle of walnut ketchup, and some horrible sweets' (Book II, Chapter 12). But if the shop is wretched, Dickens wants us to see that 'Miss Pleasant Riderhood had some little position and connection in Limehouse Hole'. She has been running this shop since her teens, and the detail of the two crossed pipes suggests pride in her business. Dolls' dressmaker Jenny Wren, 'child in years, woman in self reliance and trial', turns scraps into beautiful little dresses, and the taxidermist Mr Venus recycles humanity itself with his articulated skeletons: 'I have just sent home a Beauty—a perfect Beauty—to a school of art. One leg Belgian, one leg English, and the pickings of eight other people in it' (Book I, Chapter 7).

City working, city patterns of behaviour. Characters are often on the move, in the streets, getting to or from the next scene. Native guides can be necessary. '"We just twist up Chancery-lane"', the clerk Mr Guppy shows the way in *Bleak House*, '"and cut along Holborn, and there we are in four minutes time, as near as a toucher"' (Chapter 4). Another lawyer's clerk, Wemmick in *Great Expectations*, exemplifies the new species of urban commuter. At home genial and hospitable, at work he is 'dry and distant'. Pip decides there are 'twin Wemmicks', and when they start the commute back to the suburbs together 'we had not gone half a dozen yards down Gerrard-street in the Walworth direction before I found that I was walking arm-in-arm with the right twin, and that the wrong twin had evaporated into the evening air' (Chapter 48).

The anonymity of city life constantly strikes Dickens. In 1835 Boz reflects in his sketch 'Thoughts about People':

> It is strange with how little notice, good, bad, or indifferent, a man may live and die in London. He awakens no sympathy in the breast of any single person; his existence is a matter of interest to no one save himself; he cannot be said to be forgotten when he dies, for no one remembered him when he was alive.

Esther Summerson in *Bleak House* watches thirteen-year-old Charley Neckett run back to her work 'and melt into the city's strife and sound, like a dewdrop in an ocean' (Chapter 15). City-dwellers are in danger of losing their pasts. '"Put her in a room"', says Mr Pancks of Miss Wade in *Little Dorrit*, '"in London here with any six people old enough to be her parents, and her parents may be there for anything she knows. They may be in any house she sees, they may be in any churchyard she passes, she may run against 'em in any street, she may make chance acquaintances of 'em at any time; and never know it"' (Book II, Chapter 9).

Life on the Dickens street sets public against hidden. The public city is pleasure and consumption, display and theatre. Even the corpses in the Paris morgue in Dickens's 1856 essay 'Railway Dreaming' present themselves 'on inclined planes within a great glass window, as though Holbein should represent Death, in his grim Dance, keeping a shop, and displaying his goods like a Regent Street or Boulevard linen-draper'. (Dickens drew the line, though, at public hangings, and campaigned vociferously against them.) For him, urban is a constantly changing text, both figuratively and literally. It is a city of paper and words, print everywhere. He enjoyed interviewing the King of the Bill-Stickers for *Household Words*, the man in charge of a cavalcade of advertising vans parading through the streets, placarded with 'terrific announcements... which, being a summary of the contents of a Sunday newspaper were of the most thrilling kind'. Dickens notes the 'layers of decomposing posters' on walls and streets, and invented the term 'sandwich man'.

But behind the display is the concealed city, the dark web. 'A solemn consideration, when I enter a great city by night', wrote Dickens in *A Tale of Two Cities* in 1859, 'that every one of those darkly clustered houses encloses its own secret; that every room in every one of them encloses its own secret' (Book I, Chapter 3). Sprawling labyrinthine London crammed with seeming strangers; sprawling labyrinthine novels crammed likewise: no wonder Dickens and London sometimes seem synonymous.

The man who holds the key is another Dickens hero, described in his earliest incarnation as 'a race peculiar to the City'. This is Nadgett the detective in *Martin Chuzzlewit*.

> How he lived was a secret; where he lived was a secret; and even what he was, was a secret. In his musty old pocket-book he carried contradictory cards, in some of which he called himself a coal-merchant, in others a wine-merchant, on others a commission-agent, in others a collector, in others an accountant: as if he really didn't know the secret himself.
>
> (Chapter 27)

Once Dickens got to know and admire the real-life Inspector Field, his fictional detectives became less dingy, more commanding. 'Time and place cannot bind Mr Bucket' in *Bleak House*; a 'homely Jupiter', he acts as a guide 'descending into a deeper complication of... streets' (Chapters 53, 54, 59). *Household Words* featured many articles which extolled the merits of the new detective force, even while interpolating, in a typical Dickensian swerve, the subject position of the hunted alongside the hunters. 'To lie at night', he writes in his 1851 article 'On Duty with Inspector Field',

> wrapped in the legend of my slinking life; to take the cry that pursues me, waking, to my breast in sleep; to have it staring at me, and clamouring for me, as soon as consciousness returns... And to know that I *must* be stopped, come what will. To know that I am no match for this individual energy and keenness, or this organised and steady system!

In *Our Mutual Friend*, the Night-Inspector is commended for his ability to keep calm, 'posting up his books in a white-washed office, as studiously as if he were in a monastery on the top of a mountain, and no howling fury of a drunken woman were banging herself against a cell-door in the back-yard at his elbow' (Book I, Chapter 3). Here is the force for order in the chaos of the city.

Infernal Gulfs

For all his trips to thieves' kitchens with Inspector Field, Dickens had his own no-go areas in the city, dating back to his childhood. He 'could not endure to go near' Hungerford Stairs where the blacking factory was, he wrote in his autobiographical fragment, until the area had been redeveloped. He would cross the Strand to 'avoid a certain smell of the cement they put upon the blacking-corks, which reminded me of what I was once'. As for the Marshalsea: 'My old way home by the Borough made me cry, after my eldest child could speak.' London streets in Dickens's novels, especially for children, are fraught with danger. Out on his first errand for his benefactor Mr Brownlow, Oliver Twist is snatched back by Fagin's gang. On her first urban outing, little Florence Dombey is kidnapped by 'a very ugly old woman, with red rims round her eyes, and a mouth that mumbled and chattered of itself when she was not speaking'. She takes the child's clothes, threatening '"I could have you killed at any time"', and whips out a pair of scissors. 'Florence was so relieved to find that it was only her hair and not her head which Mrs Brown coveted' (Chapter 6).

Nowhere is the attraction of repulsion stronger for Dickens than on the streets of violence. His two historical novels have street terror at their core. *Barnaby Rudge* takes the Gordon Riots of 1780 and builds towards a climactic series of chapters mapping the nights of rioting, looting, and destruction. The combination of crowd plus London streets interests Dickens intensely: he introduces the 'mob' as 'a creature of very mysterious existence, particularly in a large city'. It is a 'creature', an elemental power. He compares it with the sea, 'for the ocean is not more fickle and uncertain, more terrible when roused, more unreasonable, or more cruel' (Chapter 52). An uncontrollable beast, it howls like wolves, it tramples, whoops, yells, swarms, roars. When Dickens says 'The noise, and hurry, and excitement, had for hundreds and hundreds an attraction they had no firmness to resist', that goes for him too. For him, the mob is hyper-exciting, hyper-destructive, and finally self-destructive. The sack of London culminates in apocalyptic scenes 'as though the last day had come and the whole universe were burning'. In their 'unappeasable and maniac rage' the rabble drink the scorching spirits running in the streets outside a vintner's house, and die terribly. With moral symmetry they 'became themselves the dust and ashes of the flames they had kindled, and strewed the public streets of London' (Chapter 68).

Two decades later, in *A Tale of Two Cities* (see Figure 6), Dickens returned to the 'dreadful spectacle' of street violence, as he had called it in *Barnaby Rudge*. This time the main event is the French Revolution, and the effects are more concentrated. The Paris district where the revolutionaries live mutates into a frightening monster with 'wild-beast thought'. 'A tremendous roar arose from the throat of Saint Antoine, and a forest of naked arms struggled in the air like shrivelled branches of trees in a winter wind' (Book II,

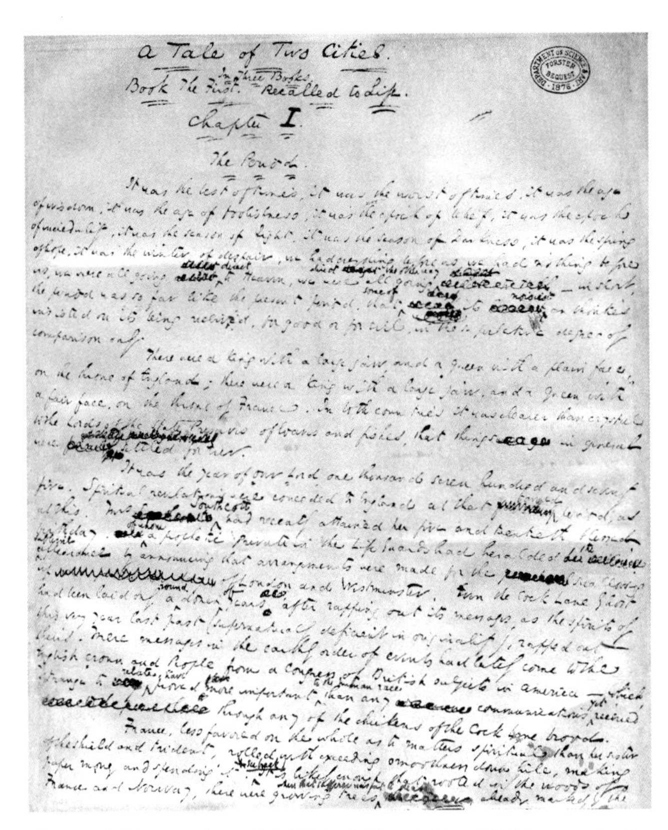
A Tale of Two Cities.

In Three Books.

Book the First. Recalled to Life.

Chapter I.

The Period.

Figure 6 Manuscript of *A Tale of Two Cities*, 1859, now in the Victoria and Albert Museum, London, and accessible online.

Chapter 21). Before Dickens, tumbrils were just two-wheeled carts; now they are defined as the gruesome vehicles which bear prisoners to execution: terror as street theatre. At the centre of the savagery is the 'one hideous figure...of the sharp female called La Guillotine'. She transfixes Dickens, and he lets rip with the gallows humour:

> It was the popular theme for jests; it was the best cure for head-ache, it infallibly prevented the hair from turning grey, it imparted a peculiar delicacy to the complexion, it was the National Razor which shaved close: who kissed La Guillotine, looked through the little window and sneezed into the sack.
>
> (Book III, Chapter 5)

The walking version of it is Madame Defarge, of all the murderous women 'not one among them more to be dreaded than this ruthless woman, now taking her way along the streets' (III.14).

The other urban terror is contagion. Poverty, pollution, and disease progressively darken the city. Dickens's early sketches and novels had abounded in slums and garrets, but by the 1850s the air of London has thickened. 'Nothing to breathe but streets, streets, streets' in *Little Dorrit* (Book I, Chapter 3). The poverty, Dickens tells us in *Bleak House*, is breeding something ominous, inhuman. The 'tumbling tenements' of Tom-all-alone's in the heart of London 'contain, by night, a swarm of misery'.

> As, on the ruined human wretch, vermin parasites appear, so, these ruined shelters have bred a crowd of foul existence that crawls in and out of gaps in walls and boards; and coils itself

> to sleep, in maggot numbers, where the rain drips in; and comes and goes, fetching and carrying fever.
>
> (Chapter 16)

Out of this 'infernal gulf' comes Jo the crossing-sweeper to infect some of the novel's cast of characters.

And pollution from the river too, that 'deadly sewer', as Dickens calls the Thames in *Little Dorrit* (Book I, Chapter 3). His last completed novel, *Our Mutual Friend*, opens on a twilight Thames of 'slime and ooze' and two characters in a filthy boat. What are they doing? The title of the first chapter, 'On the Look Out', refers to them and to us too, as we try to decipher the opaque and murky scene:

> he could not be a waterman; his boat was too crazy and too small to take in a cargo for delivery, and he could not be a lighterman or river-carrier; there was no clue to what he looked for, but he looked for something, with a most intent and searching gaze.

Their business turns out to be scavenging corpses from the river—a grisly scene to begin a novel. To this 'desert' spring brings no renewal but rather London 'at its worst. Such a black shrill city, combining the qualities of a smoky house and a scolding wife; such a gritty city; such a hopeless city, with no rent in the leaden canopy of its sky' (Book I, Chapter 12). Air texture is invasive, 'city grit gets into the hair and eyes and skin' (Book II, Chapter 15). The London fog which Dickens had used to get *Bleak House* off to a bravura start a dozen years ago is now heavier, nastier. *Bleak House's* famous opening paragraph has dogs, horses, and people all jostling one another in the fog, and fancies meeting 'a Megalosaurus, forty feet long or so, waddling like an elephantine lizard up Holborn-hill'. The 'rusty-black' fog opening Book Three of *Our Mutual Friend* brings 'smarting eyes and irritated lungs ... blinking, wheezing, and choking'. Now, disgustingly, 'the whole metropolis was a heap of vapour charged with muffled sound of wheels, and enfolding a gigantic catarrh'.

Oases

To redress some of these evils Dickens looked to practical solutions. His speeches and journalism campaigned for sanitary reforms which would cleanse the city. He supported ragged schools for the poorest children, he reported on conditions in workhouses, he expended time and energy on the young women at Urania Cottage. His novels propose other remedies: improvised bolt-holes, havens, and bulwarks against what *Our Mutual Friend* refers to as the 'sooty embrace' of the city (Book III, Chapter 1). In *The Old Curiosity Shop* Daniel Quilp invites Dick Swiveller to 'be perfectly snug and happy' drinking eye-wateringly fiery spirits in his summer-house—a space wedged in, salvaged out of the detritus of the city, 'a rugged wooden box, rotten and bare to see, which overhung the river's mud, and threatened to slide down into it' (Chapter 21). In the middle of *Little Dorrit*'s London lies Bleeding Heart Yard, inhabited by the poorest people, well-acquainted with debtors' prisons and workhouses. Even here, though, with a bit of paint and imagination, a 'perfect Pastoral' delights its owner:

> Mrs. Plornish's shop-parlor had been decorated under her own eye, and presented, on the side towards the shop, a little fiction in which Mrs. Plornish unspeakably rejoiced. This poetical heightening of the parlor consisted in the wall being painted to represent the exterior of a thatched cottage; the artist having introduced (in as effective a manner as he found compatible with their highly disproportionate dimensions) the real door and window. The modest sun-flower and holly-hock were depicted as flourishing with great luxuriance on this rustic dwelling, while a quantity of dense smoke issuing from the chimney indicated good cheer within, and also, perhaps, that it had not been lately swept.
>
> (Book II, Chapter 13)

Mrs Plornish's pride is matched by Mr Wemmick's in his 'Castle' at Walworth:

> Wemmick's house was a little wooden cottage in the midst of plots of garden, and the top of it was cut out and painted like a battery mounted with guns.
>
> 'My own doing,' said Wemmick. 'looks pretty; don't it?'
>
> I highly commended it. I think it was the smallest house I ever saw; with the queerest gothic windows (by far the greater part of them sham), and a gothic door, almost too small to get in at.
>
> 'That's a real flagstaff, you see,' said Wemmick, 'and on Sundays I run up a real flag. Then look here. After I have crossed this bridge, I hoist it up—so—and cut off the communication.'
>
> The bridge was a plank, and it crossed a chasm about four feet wide and two deep. But it was very pleasant to see the pride with which he hoisted it up and made it fast; smiling as he did so, with a relish and not merely mechanically.
>
> (Chapter 25)

Our Mutual Friend, London at its harshest, can still offer a haven at the Six Jolly Fellowship Porters,

> a bar to soften the human breast. The available space in it was not much larger than a hackney-coach; but no one could have wished the bar bigger, that space was so girt in by corpulent little casks, and by cordial-bottles radiant with fictitious grapes in bunches, and by lemons in nets, and by biscuits in baskets, and by the polite beer-pulls that made low bows when customers were served with beer, and by the cheese in a snug corner, and by the landlady's own small table in a snugger corner near the fire, with the cloth everlastingly laid.
>
> (Book I, Chapter 6)

Above the blackened rooftops and 'close dark streets', old Riah, the servant of avaricious money-lender Fledgeby, has created a little garden where two young women, Lizzie Hexam and Jenny Wren, can find peace. '"Such a chain has fallen from you, and such a strange good sorrowful happiness comes upon you"', says Jenny, when she is up here. '"Come back and be dead"', she calls to Riah—as if the price of escape from the city is death (Book II, Chapter 5). Dickens's last novel, *The Mystery of Edwin Drood*, delves into the most wretched areas of London, the drug-dens by the docks. Once again solace is at hand at attic level, with the window boxes of mignonette and wallflower, and ingenious lines for scarlet runner beans, rigged up by ship-shape sailor Mr Tartar. Gardeners get Dickens's approval, and urban gardeners especially. His own favourite flower was the red geranium: cheap and colourful pot-plant, townsman's miniature oasis.

The Dickens city, then, has its retreats, it has its fears and excitements, its rhythms and patterns of behaviour. And threading through every novel are the streets to be negotiated by powerful and powerless alike. This is where we leave Little Dorrit and her new husband in the closing words of the novel:

> They went quietly down into the roaring streets, inseparable and blessed; and as they passed along in sunshine and in shade, the noisy and the eager, and the arrogant and the froward and the vain, fretted, and chafed, and made their usual uproar.

5

Radical Dickens

In the last year of his life Dickens ended a public speech with the declaration: 'My faith in the people governing, is, on the whole, infinitesimal; my faith in The People governed, is, on the whole, illimitable.' He was a life-long radical. According to Forster, it was Dickens's childhood experiences which instilled 'the hatred of oppression, the revolt against abuse of power, and the war with injustice under every form'. Dickens would unfailingly take the side of the poor and the underdog. 'Certainly a subversive writer,' as George Orwell put it, 'Dickens attacked English institutions with a ferocity that has never since been approached.' His vision darkened with age, but although his focus changed, the radicalism never left him.

Early Targets and Sledge-Hammer Blows

Arranging all his Boz sketches to best advantage for their reissue in 1837, Dickens chose to start with a sequence 'From Our Parish'—Parish meaning local government and its administration. Here are the opening sentences:

> How much is conveyed in those two short words—'The Parish'! And with how many tales of distress and misery, or broken fortune and ruined hope, too often of unrelieved wretchedness and successful knavery, are they associated!

The persona Dickens constructs as the curtain goes up on his career is Boz the friend of the poor, their champion against unfeeling and untrustworthy authority. A year later *Oliver Twist*, subtitled *The Parish Boy's Progress*, took the fight to one state institution in particular: the workhouses where the state warehoused—and abused—the orphaned, the poor, the elderly and infirm, breaking up families in the process.

For his next novel, *Nicholas Nickleby*, Dickens picked another visible manifestation of cruelty to children: the private schools in Yorkshire. 'I have kept down the strong truth', Dickens told a friend after his research trip for *Nicholas Nickleby*, 'and thrown as much comicality over it as I could, rather than disgust and weary the reader with its fouler aspects.' These schools, which advertised 'no holidays', were dumping grounds for inconvenient children far away from friends and family. In Dickens's hands, Dotheboys Hall is a freezing lair of beatings and starvation, presided over by the ogre Wackford Squeers. He can boast a convincing pedagogic veneer:

> 'We go upon the practical mode of teaching, Nickleby; the regular education system. C-l-e-a-n, clean, verb active, to make bright, to scour. W-i-n, win, d-e-r, der, winder, a casement. When this boy knows this out of the book, he goes and does it.'
>
> (Chapter 8)

But while his sadism may seem pantomime—'"I never thrashed a boy in a hackney-coach before," said Mr Squeers, when he stopped to rest. "There's inconveniency in it, but the novelty gives it a sort of relish too!"' (Chapter 38)—Dickens makes his hero as angry as he wants his readers to be, when he defies Squeers for beating the helpless Smike. 'Nicholas sprang upon him, wrested the weapon from his hand, and, pinning him by the throat, beat the ruffian till he roared for mercy.' But then high-minded justice, in typical Dickensian about-turn, yields to knockabout as Squeers's daughter Fanny joins in, 'and after launching a shower of inkstands at the usher's head, beat Nicholas to her heart's content, animating herself at every blow with the recollection of his having refused her proffered love' (Chapter 13).

Dickens had republican views, as his *Child's History of England* makes abundantly obvious with its superfluity of bad kings and queens—a Horrible History with Alfred the Great as a rare honourable exception. When republican America failed to live up to his expectations he makes Martin Chuzzlewit's visit there a comic catastrophe. But his Preface to the novel suggests that his vision is now opening out, his 'main object' being 'to show how Selfishness propagates itself; and to what a grim giant it may grow, from small beginnings'. The story he wrote between instalments of *Martin Chuzzlewit* marked him forever as torch-bearer for the poor. '"This boy is Ignorance"' declaims the Ghost of Christmas Present. '"This girl is Want. Beware them both, and all of their degree, but most of all beware this boy, for on his brow I see that written which is Doom, unless the writing be erased"' (Stave III). *A Christmas Carol* pits this stark prediction against the optimistic hope that the writing of Doom—a fitting metaphor for a crusading novelist—can be erased by the writing of reform. Here and in his next Christmas book, *The Chimes*, 'he was bent', according to Forster, 'on striking a blow for the poor'. And as he got into the stride of his public persona he enjoyed landing what he called sledge-hammer blows on behalf of the cause of the moment. To do so, he could choose from a variety of media.

In the hundreds of public speeches he gave throughout his career he could carry the banner in person. His journalism and letters to the national press denounced abuses such as child labour down the coal-mines, cholera-ridden baby farms, and public hangings, in tones ranging from scathing satire to outraged civic indignation. The founding of *Household Words* in 1850 gave him a regular platform, as some of the titles he contemplated for it suggest: *The Lever, The Forge, The Crucible, The Anvil of Time.* Throughout the 1850s his magazine addressed important and controversial issues: factory conditions, slum housing, public health and hygiene, women's employment, education, emigration, crime and prison discipline, government bureaucracy and administration.

The workhouse bugbear persisted in both journalism and fiction. Old Nandy in *Little Dorrit* is immured 'in a grove of two score and nineteen more old men, every one of whom smells of all the others' (Book I, Chapter 31). So terrified is the old washerwoman Betty Higden in *Our Mutual Friend* of being 'brick[ed] up in the Unions' (the workhouse) that she flees her home, 'trudging through the streets, away from paralysis and pauperism' towards freedom and death (Book II, Chapter 14). 'Worn-out old people of low estate', comments Dickens high on his satirical horse, 'have a trick of reasoning as indifferently as they live, and doubtless would appreciate our Poor Law more philosophically on an income of ten thousand a year' (Book III, Chapter 9). The voice of protester on behalf of the people suited him. He liked feeling embattled. 'I have fought the fight across the Atlantic with the utmost energy I could command', he wrote to the English publisher Thomas Longman about international copyright in 1842; 'have never been turned aside by any consideration for an instant; am fresher for the fray than ever; will battle it to the death, and die game to the last.'

Broader, Darker

As Britain and her empire swelled in size and confidence, Dickens's own belief in it diminished. For him the best of times were becoming the worst of times, Victorian high noon was dusk verging on midnight. Not that he was anti-progress. As Ruskin aptly said, 'Dickens was a pure modernist—a leader of the steam-whistle party par excellence.' The titles he chose for fake book-jackets adorning his study door at Gad's Hill succinctly express his attitude to the past: *The Wisdom of Our Ancestors* in seven volumes: 1 *Ignorance*, 2 *Superstition*, 3 *The Block*, 4 *The Stake*, 5 *The Rack*, 6 *Dirt*, 7 *Disease*. Articles in *Household Words* toured readers round modern factories and communication centres such as the General Post Office. But by the 1850s, rather than highlighting an issue like the workhouse or a vice like selfishness,

Dickens was organizing his novels around his critique of the dehumanizing structures, ideologies, and bureaucracies of nineteenth-century Britain.

Dickens began work on *Bleak House* in 1851—the year of the Great Exhibition, showcase to the world for the wonders of industrial Britain. Dickens was less sure of the wonders of his nation. *Bleak House* was the first of a run of three novels (*Hard Times* and *Little Dorrit* followed) to tackle Britain's ruling institutions and attitudes. His primary target in *Bleak House* is the legal system, exemplified by the incomprehensible and interminable Jarndyce lawsuit. 'The little plaintiff or defendant,' the narrator tells us in the opening chapter,

> who was promised a new rocking-horse when Jarndyce and Jarndyce should be settled, has grown up, possessed himself of a real horse, and trotted away into the other world.
>
> (Chapter 1)

Those effortless transitions between horses real, rocking, and incorporeal, and between 'this world and the next': what precipitous dimensions they open up. The whole first chapter dazzles with its giddying shifts of scale expanding and contracting, converging and radiating, from the real fog of London to the 'foggy glory' of the Chancellor's wig and out to the 'blighted land in every shire'. All involved in the legal system are doomed. The 'ruined suitor, who periodically appears from Shropshire' and tries to address the Chancellor directly, face-to-face, has become a figure of fun. '"There again!" said Mr Gridley, with no diminution of his rage. "The system! I am told on all hands, it's the system. I mustn't look to individuals. It's the system"' (Chapter 1).

If 'The one great principle of the English law is, to make business for itself' (Chapter 39), other institutions are equally culpable. Religion, in the shape of the clergyman Mr Chadband, is self-regarding, greedy, and greasy. 'A large yellow man with a fat smile and a general appearance of having a good deal of train oil in his system', he spouts 'abominable nonsense' (Chapter 19). Philanthropy, as embodied in Mrs Jellyby, is looking the wrong way, towards Africa instead of the inner city. The aristocracy, exemplified by Sir Leicester Dedlock, is 'intensely prejudiced, perfectly unreasonable' (Chapter 2). As George Bernard Shaw commented in his 1937 Foreword to *Great Expectations*, 'Trollope and Thackeray could see Chesney Wold [where the Dedlocks live]; but Dickens could see through it.' And that central institution of care and protection, the family itself, proves woefully inadequate. Everywhere in the book are abandoned, neglected, and exploited children, and some appalling parenting. The legal system, it becomes clear, is metonymic, synecdoche for something rotten in the state, the rottenness of the state itself. This is the prosperous nation which cannot educate its children, cannot look after its poor, cannot keep its cities clean, and cannot bury its dead properly.

In this vexed world there are no simple solutions. Quietism, staying as aloof as possible, is the path chosen by John Jarndyce as he provides succour to the defenceless. But his scope is limited, and his unworldliness lays him open to being duped, for instance by the calculatingly irresponsible 'I'm just a child' Harold Skimpole. It is, surprisingly, the cottagey haven Mr Jarndyce establishes outside London to protect his young wards, which is called Bleak House, and where Esther becomes infected with the smallpox coming out of the London slum. So it turns out that there is no good place in this novel which is un-bleak.

The form of the novel re-enforces the sense of disequilibrium, with its two modes of narration fitting uneasily together. One is the omniscient third-person narrator using the historic present. The other is the past tense and first person of Esther Summerson contributing 'my portion of these pages' (Chapter 3). Her portion could have taken the form of letter or journal; her words suggest that she is collaborating with someone, but with whom? The novel is an experiment in destabilization, constructing a multiplicity of viewpoints, not one of which is privileged. Its final paragraph finishes mid-sentence in uncertainty, as Esther wonders '—even supposing—. ' So right to its end this mammoth novel will not settle down; it resists closure, and throws open the 'system' of the novel.

Further contributing to the unease is the anxiety about literacy brooding throughout. What is it like not to be able to read or write? An illustration of Jo the illiterate crossing-sweeper occupies the titlepage of the first single-volume edition of the novel, slumped outside the Society for the Propagation of the Gospel in Foreign Parts. He is at the bottom of society, and in an extraordinary passage the narrator thinks himself into Jo's subject position:

> To see people read, and to see people write, and to see the postmen deliver letters, and not to have the least idea of all

> that language—to be, to every scrap of it, stone blind and dumb!... what does it all mean, and if it means anything to anybody, how comes it that it means nothing to me?
>
> (Chapter 16)

And there is so much of 'all that unaccountable reading and writing' needed to keep London going, 'the great tee-totum... set up for its daily spin and whirl'. Indeed, far too much of it, over-literacy possibly as bad as illiteracy.

Writing is the default position of many characters, much to their disadvantage. People are always at it, characters dwindle into its constituent elements. '"I am only pen and ink to *her*"' sobs the exasperated Caddy Jellyby (Chapter 14), enforced amanuensis for her mother's philanthropic mania. Others, like Richard Carstone and the lawyer Tulkinghorn, are in danger of drying up and turning into paper; paper is in danger of turning into litter: in Mrs Jellyby's cluttered cupboards, in mad Miss Flite's reticule, in Krook's filthy rag-and-bone shop, in the law courts. Dickens himself at this time seems to have been feeling the need to be more present to his readers. *Household Words*, founded in the year before he started *Bleak House*, was his attempt to speak directly to a larger audience. He was on the verge of a new career as a reader of his novels; never was he more in demand as a public speaker. Face-to-face is what he values, and the novel mounts an offensive against writing, in writing—all nine hundred pages of it.

To transcend the novel's 'writtenness' Dickens draws on the rhetorical flourish of the speaking voice: the prophecy of the avenging slum-dwellers in Tom-all-alone's—'not an atom of Tom's slime...but shall work its retribution through every order of society'—and the scalding apostrophe of the elegy for Jo which disrupts plot and form to exhort us directly: 'Dead, your Majesty. Dead, my lords and gentlemen. Dead, Right Reverends and Wrong Reverends of every order. Dead, men and women, born with Heavenly compassion in your hearts. And dying thus around us, every day' (Chapter 47).

Hard Times, Dickens's next and shortest novel, moves the battle on. It is dedicated to his friend and mentor, Thomas Carlyle, who had analysed the nation's ills in 'Signs of the Times' (1829): 'Men are grown mechanical in head and in heart, as well as in hand.' Or, as Dickens ascribes it to his representative of utilitarianism in his novel:

> It was a fundamental principle of the Gradgrind philosophy that everything was to be paid for. Nobody was ever on any account to give anybody anything, or render anybody help without purchase. Gratitude was to be abolished, and the virtues springing from it were not to be. Every inch of the existence of mankind, from birth to death, was to be a bargain across a counter. And if we didn't get to Heaven that way, it was not a politico-economical place, and we had no business there.
>
> (Book III, Chapter 8)

The *Hard Times* parable proposes a stark opposition between this world and the next, between economic man and the Christian values and beliefs which Dickens consistently upheld throughout his life.

Moving outside London for once, he goes north, mapping his attack on utilitarian philosophy onto the landscape of the industrialized workforce. For this new environment new words are needed. The Coketown people are 'workful'; the shrubberies in the suburban gardens are 'besmoked'. 'The Key-Note' chapter makes the point:

> Fact, fact, fact, everywhere in the material aspect of the town; fact, fact, fact, everywhere in the immaterial... everything was fact between the lying-in hospital and the cemetery, and what you couldn't state in figures, or show to be purchaseable in the cheapest market and saleable in the dearest, was not, and never should be, world without end, Amen.
>
> (Book I, Chapter 5)

Set within this frame of 'world without end', the language of materialism becomes a blasphemous liturgy. The stakes could not be higher.

At the heart of *Hard Times* is the issue of education. '"Go and be somethingological directly"', Mrs Gradgrind tells her children (Book I, Chapter 4). '"Now, what I want is, Facts. Teach these boys and girls nothing but Facts. Facts alone are wanted in life"' are the first words of the book and central to Mr Gradgrind's 'system' as he calls it later, when ruing its consequences for his children. '"I have meant to do right"', he says, with a commentary from Dickens to ensure that we do not make him the villain of the piece.

> He said it earnestly, and to do him justice he had. In gauging fathomless deeps with his little mean excise-rod, and in staggering over the universe with his rusty stiff-legged compasses, he had meant to do great things. Within the limits of his short tether he had tumbled about, annihilating the flowers of

> existence with greater singleness of purpose than many of the blatant personages whose company he kept.
>
> (Book III, Chapter 1)

Although Mr Gradgrind sees the error of his ways Dickens has no faith in the Parliament where Gradgrind sits as an MP doing any good—the 'cinderheap', the 'national dustyard' as he calls it. Rather, it is Dickens's prose which comes to the rescue. The novel is, appropriately, suffused with 'fanciful imagination', Dickens's prime weapon in his assault on the dead hand of utilitarian thinking. His imagery casts the chimneys and steam engines of Coketown into interminable serpents and melancholy mad elephants. Violence simmers beneath the sullen surfaces of the Gradgrind children. Tom wants to '"put a thousand barrels of gunpowder"' under all the Facts and Figures '"and blow them all up together!"' (Book I, Chapter 8); Louisa watches for the fire which 'bursts out' of the factory chimneys at night (Book I, Chapter 15).

Throughout the book Dickens switches between smoke-blackened Coketown and the eternal perspectives of the 'laws of Creation', between the tethered goat Gradgrind and the universe he staggers over with his compasses, between 'the utmost cunning of algebra' and 'the last trumpet ever to be sounded [which] shall blow even algebra to wreck' (Book I, Chapter 15). The voice of the prophet is heard again, reinforcing the book's Biblical language and cadences with warnings to us to heed the needs of working people or 'Reality will take a wolfish turn, and make an end of you!' (Book II, Chapter 6).

Dickens's initial idea for his next novel was, according to Forster, of 'a leading man for a story who should bring about all the mischief in it, lay it all on Providence, and say at every fresh calamity, "nobody was to blame"'; the title was to be *Nobody's Fault*. But Dickens soon had more topical targets in his sights, and many to cast at fault—in fact a whole system. 'I have relieved my indignant soul with a scarifier,' he told his friend Wilkie Collins while planning *Little Dorrit* in 1855. The book's tenth chapter, 'Containing the Whole Science of Government', goes for the jugular in its first paragraph:

> The Circumlocution Office was (as everybody knows without being told) the most important Department under government. No public business of any kind could possibly be done at any time, without the acquiescence of the Circumlocution Office. Its finger was in the largest public pie, and in the smallest public tart. It was equally impossible to do the plainest right and to undo the plainest wrong, without the express authority of the Circumlocution Office. If another Gunpowder Plot had been discovered half an hour before the lighting of the match, nobody would have been justified in saving the parliament until there had been half a score of boards, half a bushel of minutes, several sacks of official memoranda, and a family-vault-full of ungrammatical correspondence, on the part of the Circumlocution Office.

Circumlocution: the paragraph lands us where we started, mimicking the circularity of the system. Its great watchword is 'HOW NOT TO DO IT', meaning how to do nothing about anything, so that in an appropriately swollen and higgledy-piggledy list:

> Mechanicians, natural philosophers, soldiers, sailors, petitioners, memorialists, people with grievances, people who

> wanted to prevent grievances, people who wanted to redress grievances, jobbing people, jobbed people, people who couldn't get rewarded for merit, and people who couldn't get punished for demerit, were all indiscriminately tucked up under the foolscap paper of the Circumlocution Office.

Dickens's diatribe against civil-service bureaucracy was timely: an enquiry into the conduct of the Crimean War was revealing gross administrative incompetence. For the only time in his life he joined a political movement, the Administrative Reform Association.

As Dickens tells it, the Circumlocution Office is in the hands of one family, the Tite Barnacles. In his quest to help the bankrupt Mr Dorrit Arthur Clennam is cheerfully given masses of forms to fill in—'"You can have a dozen, if you like"'—but no hope of success. Barnacles can be likeable, even while understanding 'the Department to be a politico-diplomatic hocus pocus piece of machinery' (Book I, Chapter 10). Lifting his gaze from the miles of 'red tape' which could 'stretch, in graceful festoons, from Hyde Park corner to the General Post Office' (Book II, Chapter 8), Dickens indicts the whole 'Barnacle tribe', the governing class and all its hangers on, clinging on across the empire. 'The paternal Gowan', for example (father of the charlatan artist Henry—Dickens detests artists who are not serious about their work),

> originally attached to a legation abroad, had been pensioned off as a Commissioner of nothing particular somewhere or other, and had died at his post with his drawn salary in his hand, nobly defending it to the last extremity.
>
> (Book I, Chapter 18)

Henry's mother has been given lodgings in Hampton Court Palace, along with 'several other old ladies of both sexes', where she entertains tribe members such as Lord Lancaster Stiltstalking, the 'noble Refrigerator' who

> had iced several European courts in his time, and had done it with such complete success that the very name of Englishman yet struck cold to the stomachs of foreigners who had the distinguished honor of remembering him, at a distance of a quarter of a century.
>
> (Book I, Chapter 26)

Dickens invariably directs his fire against those who wield power badly, be they petty officials, cruel judges, or the aristocracy, though in his own personal dealings with the latter he could be obsequious. Now the class system comes into focus as the cause of the country's ills. *Little Dorrit* is, according to George Bernard Shaw, 'a more seditious book than *Das Kapital*'. The theme rumbles through the novel and surfaces in satirical parallels, such as William Dorrit, imprisoned for debt in the Marshalsea and massaging his self-esteem by patronizing the workhouse resident Old Nandy:

> Mr. Dorrit was in the habit of receiving this old man, as if the old man held of him in vassalage under some feudal tenure. He made little treats and teas for him, as if he came in with his homage from some outlying district where the tenantry were in a primitive state.
>
> (Book I, Chapter 31)

William Dorrit is in prison; and this is the novel's dark and controlling image for a society enchained by class and ideology. At last the Marshalsea can find its place in Dickens's fiction, to embody the mental, social, and spiritual structures which Dickens shows to be so constricting. From the educational philosophy of the governess Mrs General, whose 'ways of forming a mind—to cram all articles of difficulty into cupboards, lock them up, and say they had no existence' (Book II, Chapter 2), to the fierce Old Testament religion of Arthur's mother, with her bible 'bound like her own construction of it in the hardest, barest, and straitest boards, with one dinted ornament on the cover like the drag of a chain, and a wrathful sprinkling of red upon the edges of the leaves' (Book I, Chapter 3): this is a book full of things and people locked and shut up.

Antidotes, Homes, Carnivals

So far, so bleak. But relief is at hand. Dickens's rage against the system can be violent: prisons are burnt down in *Barnaby Rudge* and flung open in *A Tale of Two Cities*. In *Bleak House* the illiterate Krook is nicknamed the Lord Chancellor. His crazy shop is a parody Chancery and his death by spontaneous combustion the author's vengeful desire to put a bomb under the whole Chancery system. But such explosions are rare. Dickens was not one to advocate anarchy. He looks rather to the antidotes and respites afforded by safe spaces and interludes of carnival. Where he likes to be best is in the family circle round the fireside. When 'all the Cratchit family drew round the hearth, in what Bob Cratchit called a circle, meaning half a one' (Stave III), Dickens installed himself there too. Think of yourselves as 'a group of friends, listening to a tale told by a winter fire', he urged the audience at his public reading of *A Christmas Carol* in 1858. 'No man', wrote his daughter Mamie, 'was so inclined naturally to derive his happiness from home affairs. He was full of the kind of interest in a house which is commonly confined to women.' His own houses often feature in his letters, with precise directions for home improvements including designs for shower curtains.

Home, rather than pastoral Eden or heavenly city, is the great good place for Dickens, its locations many and various. It can be in a thieves' den like Fagin's, in shops like the Wooden Midshipman in *Dombey and Son*, or legal chambers like Mr Grewgious's in *Edwin Drood*. Characters who can create havens, however temporary, are celebrated. An improvised trim interior is best (Dickens was a demon for tidiness, as his children knew only too well), diminutive and tight against the world outside. Mrs Jarley's caravan in *The Old Curiosity Shop*, 'not a shabby, dingy, dusty cart, but a smart little house upon wheels, with white dimity curtains festooning the windows, and window-shutters of green picked out with panels of a staring red, in which happily-contrasted colours the whole concern shone brilliant', offers Little Nell a harbour where she eats well and sleeps late (Chapter 26). Mr Peggotty's boat on the beach at Yarmouth charms young David Copperfield instantly. 'After tea, when the door was shut and all was made snug (the nights being cold and misty now), it seemed to me the most delicious retreat that the imagination of man could conceive' (Chapter 3). Even a prison can have its safe spots, such as the Marshalsea Snuggery's 'social evening club' in *Little Dorrit* (Book I, Chapter 8).

The shibboleths of home do not escape mockery. In *Our Mutual Friend*, Bella Wilfer takes on 'The Complete British Family Housewife' from which she is learning to cook, retorting '"Oh you ridiculous old thing, what do you mean by that? You must have been drinking!"' (Book IV, Chapter 5). It can be a place of secrets, mystery, and suffering. But home is always to be aspired to, longed for. The shut-out child is a powerful Dickens figure. The rejected Florence Dombey is, as her father recognizes belatedly, 'the spirit of his home' (Chapter 35).

These refuges, though, are susceptible to contamination and destruction. From inside Mrs Jarley's caravan, Nell glimpses Quilp pursuing her and dreams fearfully of him. Mr Peggotty's boat is blown down by the storm at the end of the book. On being deceived by his servant in *Dombey and Son*, Captain Cuttle laments the 'treachery' in the parlour 'which was a kind of sacred place' (Chapter 39). And while Dickens is second to none in his worship at the familial hearth, few of his families are happy, and many are dysfunctional. He prefers the improvised to the biological sort. Old Sol Gills and Captain Cuttle are surrogate parents for Florence Dombey. Mr Peggotty brings together children and widows left orphaned and bereft by the sea. Mr Jarndyce opens his home to illegitimate Esther Summerson and the wards in Chancery, children adrift in the legal system.

Homes, families—and entertainment. If there is a prison in almost every novel, there is also a theatre. An avid theatre-goer and zealous manager of his own amateur company,

Dickens dispatches even his demurest heroines, Agnes Wickfield and Esther Summerson, to enjoy themselves at the theatre. The youthful Nicholas Nickleby excels as actor/dramatist in a novel thronged with characters acting on and off stage. All forms of popular culture had attractions for Dickens, and melodrama in particular. It is also what many have deplored in his work. Ruskin, who considered *Hard Times* a great book, nevertheless criticized Dickens for writing in a 'circle of stage fire'. But for Dickens, all 'The Amusements of the People', as he called them in two *Household Words* essays, were to be valued. Puppet shows, Punch and Judy, and waxworks had the added charm of playing across the boundaries of animate and inanimate. Running counter to the mechanization of thought, word, and deed in *Hard Times* is Sleary's circus and horse-riding. Dickens admires both what they do—'"People must be amuthed, Thquire, thomehow"', the lisping 'never sober and never drunk' Mr Sleary tells Mr Gradgrind—and how they do it. The circus people possess 'a remarkable gentleness . . . and an untiring readiness to help and pity one another' (Book I, Chapter 6).

For all his admiration—perhaps because of it—Dickens is equally drawn to the underside of carnival. In *The Old Curiosity Shop* he shows us the Punch and Judy puppets being mended, 'all slack and drooping in a dark box', and the commerce at its heart. Mr Vuffin the giant-keeper expounds his economic 'policy':

> 'What becomes of the old giants?' said Short, turning to him again after a little reflection.

'They're usually kept in carawans to wait upon the dwarfs,' said Mr Vuffin.

'The maintaining of 'em must come expensive, when they can't be shown, eh?' remarked Short, eyeing him doubtfully.

'It's better that, than letting 'em go upon the parish or about the streets,' said Mr Vuffin. 'Once make a giant common and giants will never draw again. Look at wooden legs. If there was only one man with a wooden leg what a property *he*'d be!'

'So he would!' observed the landlord and Short both together. 'That's very true.'

'Instead of which,' pursued Mr Vuffin, 'if you was to advertise Shakespeare played entirely by wooden legs, it's my belief you wouldn't draw a sixpence.'

(Chapter 19)

Celebrating the individual and the eccentric, Dickensian carnival can take many shapes and forms. The stout elderly gent in Dickens's first novel arrives as a force of nature—indeed, *the* force of nature:

> That punctual servant of all work, the sun, had just risen... when Mr. Samuel Pickwick burst like another sun from his slumbers, threw open his chamber window, and looked out upon the world beneath.
>
> (Chapter 2)

The princes of this world are the enjoyers of life. Easy enough for men of leisure like Pickwick, gallivanting round the country with his chums; more special is the starving young servant in *The Old Curiosity Shop* who forages for scraps after her employers have gone to bed. She salvages '"pieces of orange peel to put into cold water and make believe it was wine... If you make believe very much, it's quite nice," said the small servant; "but if you don't, you know, it seems as if it would bear a little more seasoning, certainly"' (Chapter 64).

Dickens's child characters are blessed with a Wordsworthian access to the life of the imagination, and that spirit which prompts them to pose fundamental questions. '"What is money?"' asks little Paul Dombey (Chapter 8). If it '"can do anything"' as his father claims, why could it not keep his mother alive? David Copperfield admires those who retain the child's 'faculty' in later years, and so does his creator. The nurturing of this force of the imagination was the avowed mission of his new journal in 1850:

> No mere utilitarian spirit, no iron binding of the mind to grim realities, will give a harsh tone to our Household Words. In the bosoms of the young and old, of the well-to-do and of the poor, we would tenderly cherish that light of Fancy which is inherent in the human breast.

Hence Dickens's lifelong preoccupation with non-rational states of mind, with madness, with dreams, hallucinations, and semi-conscious states. He took a keen interest in mesmerism; in Italy he successfully hypnotized a fellow hotel guest suffering from nervous disorder (he had to stop when Catherine objected to his visiting a lady's bedroom at midnight). A 'night-fancy' prompts him to 'wander by Bethlehem Hospital', the lunatic asylum, for his 1860 'Night Walks' essay, as he meditates on the porous boundaries and definitions of sanity.

> Are not the sane and the insane equal at night as the sane lie a dreaming? Are not all of us outside this hospital, who dream,

> more or less in the condition of those inside it, every night of our lives? Are we not nightly persuaded, as they daily are, that we associate preposterously with kings and queens, emperors and empresses, and notabilities of all sorts? Do we not nightly jumble events and personages, and times and places, as these do daily?

His books abound with characters who are irrational, excitable, obsessed, compulsive, deluded. He takes pleasure in creating the malign demented Mrs F's Aunt in *Little Dorrit*, who terrifies Arthur Clennam with her ferocious pronouncements—'"Give him a meal of chaff"' (Book II, Chapter 9)—as well as the benignly 'childish' Mr Dick, whose advice is treasured by Betsey Trotwood. '"What shall I do with him?"' she asks when her little nephew David Copperfield turns up ragged and filthy, having run away from his wretched employment (Chapter 13). Mr Dick's practical '"I should wash him!"' has the inevitable consequence of Miss Trotwood's taking David in and, ultimately, adopting him.

Above all, Dickens relishes the fabricators and visionaries, those who can afford to be lavish with language if with nothing else. Old Mrs Gamp in *Martin Chuzzlewit*—when she appears 'a peculiar fragrance was borne upon the breeze, as if a passing fairy had hiccupped, and had previously been to a wine vaults' (Chapter 25)—has an inventive idiolect appropriate to her work as midwife and layer-out of corpses. She likes to remember children 'playing at berryins down in the shop, and follerin' the order-book to its long home in the iron safe', and is, like Dickens, a creator of character.

> A fearful mystery surrounded this lady of the name of Harris, whom no one in the circle of Mrs. Gamp's acquaintance had

> ever seen; neither did any human being know her place of residence, though Mrs. Gamp appeared on her own showing to be in constant communication with her. There were conflicting rumours on the subject; but the prevalent opinion was that she was a phantom of Mrs. Gamp's brain—as Messrs. Doe and Roe are fictions of the law—created for the express purpose of holding visionary dialogues with her on all manner of subjects, and invariably winding up with a compliment to the excellence of her nature.
>
> (Chapter 25)

Dickens's own 'visionary dialogues', his extravagant conceits and metaphysical yokings together of the totally disparate, his wilful category confusions of animate and inanimate, his extended and jumbled lists and his exuberant wordplay: for him it is ultimately the carnival of language itself which will defy the 'grim realities' and the 'iron binding of the mind' he saw all around him.

6

Dickensian

He became an adjective in his own lifetime. The Oxford English Dictionary cites 1856 for its first appearance. As we might expect, contradictions beset the many connotations of 'Dickensian'—the best and the worst. On one hand conviviality and good cheer; on the other oppression, injustice, poverty, and urban squalor. He often functions as an intensifier. A Dickensian fog, for example, is a very thick one. The meanings accruing around 'Dickensian' also have to do with his manner of writing, increasingly pejorative as what Henry James labelled the 'large loose baggy monsters' of Victorian fiction fell out of fashion. But Dickensian energy is something which always attracts. The Dickens phenomenon is partly about wanting to enjoy the fellowship whether real or virtual, and participate in the genial flow.

Christmas

Dickens is so tied to Christmas that when he died, a barrow-girl in Covent Garden market is supposed to have exclaimed, 'Then will Father Christmas die too?' In the twenty-first century, Dickens Christmas fairs, villages, and shows show no signs of abating, and it was in his own repertoire from the start. His essay 'Christmas Festivities' was published in December 1835 and has many of the constituent props already in place. 'There seems a magic in the very name of Christmas', writes Boz, with its warming fire, turkey, gigantic pudding, plum-cake, mistletoe, free-flowing wine and punch, gregarious family party, games, comic songs, and children dashing about—'a confused din of talking, laughing, and merriment' bordering on anarchy. Riotous tricks include 'the astonishing feat of pouring lighted brandy into mince pies'. There is also the scene of conversion and reconciliation. Grandmamma has been hard on grand-daughter Margaret who 'married a poor man without her consent'. Now grandmamma thaws and harmony prevails. 'Social feelings are awakened': the sketch is framed in the present tense. This is an annually recurring event with its traditions and customs, and its hope that the Christmas spirit will last all year.

Dickens himself quickly revived it; for who could better enjoy and embody the spirit of Christmas than jovial rubicund Mr Pickwick in the melée under the mistletoe, 'now pulled this way, and then that, and first kissed on the chin and then on the nose, and then on the spectacles' (Chapter 28). The Christmas pilgrimage Pickwick and his friends make from the city to the country idyll of Dingley Dell is again cast in the continuous present. The frosty jingling stagecoach journey (the railway had arrived by 1837 but not for Pickwick) fosters the important mood of 'pleasant anticipation'. More props assemble: carols, country dancing, goblin tales by the fireside, and snow, as there had been for the first eight Christmases of Dickens's childhood. And even more alcohol, some of it glorified by the name of 'wassail'. Mr Pickwick's host, Mr Wardle, talks of the 'invariable custom' of their Christmas Eve supper, when servants and employers sit down together. What is remarkable is the way in which the urban Pickwick group can be brought easily into the world of long-established traditions. Instant nostalgia, ready-made.

These are the antecedents for what was to become Dickens's best-known and most frequently adapted work, familiar to many long before they can read a word of it. But *A Christmas Carol* also had two more immediate prompts. In March 1843 Dickens's friend, the physician and sanitary reformer Thomas Southwood Smith, sent him a copy of his report for the Children's Employment Commission, which revealed many children under the age of seven to be working up to twelve hours a day and with no legal protection. It also laid bare the atrocious physical state of the children and their lack of any education. Telling Southwood Smith he was 'perfectly stricken down' by the report, Dickens thought of writing 'a very cheap pamphlet, called "An appeal to the People of England, on behalf of the Poor Man's Child"—with my name attached, of course'. Four days later he decided to defer production 'until the end of the year', reassuring Southwood Smith that 'you will certainly feel that a Sledge hammer has come down with twenty times the force—twenty thousand times the force—I could exert by following out my first idea'.

The timing of *A Christmas Carol* was superb. The early 1840s saw a surge in celebrating the season, partly due to

Victoria and Albert's enthusiasm. Christmas trees, cards, and crackers all arrived at this time. But these were also the hungry forties, a time of economic depression and famine. In September 1843 Dickens visited the Field Lane Ragged School, a charity school in the slums, and told Angela Burdett Coutts he had 'seldom seen . . . anything so shocking as the dire neglect of soul and body exhibited in these children'. Here, he predicted, 'in the prodigious misery and ignorance of the swarming masses of mankind in England, the seeds of its certain ruin are sown'. In October he spoke in Manchester on behalf of popular education. On his return and between the monthly numbers of *Martin Chuzzlewit* he launched himself on his new project, writing it in no more than a month or so. Over it, he told a friend, he 'wept, and laughed, and wept again . . . in a most extraordinary manner'.

The other spur was personal and just as pressing. Dickens was in debt, and the relatively low sales of *Martin Chuzzlewit* led to his publishers threatening to reduce their monthly payments to him by £50, as they were legally entitled to do. So Dickens was looking for a financial hit, and to begin with he was to be badly disappointed. This was his own fault. Although the *Carol* was, as he boasted, 'a most prodigious success', he had insisted on such high production values for the book—gilt on the cover, hand-coloured illustrations (a Christmas present just to look at)—that the profit for the first edition of £250 left him 'utterly knocked down' with dismay. 'I had set my heart and soul upon a Thousand, clear.' But the *Carol* soon proved it had a life of its own, reversing the usual trajectory whereby a folk-tale gets transmitted orally and then written down. Almost at one bound the *Carol* entered the public mythos, where it has remained ever since. Within a little more than a fortnight of its publication in December 1843 a pirate version appeared. For once in his life Dickens took legal action, winning his case but having to pay the pirate's expenses when he went bankrupt (the echoes reverberated in *Bleak House*). By February 1844 there were at least eight unauthorized stage productions. Dickens saw one, 'better than usual', he told Forster, 'but *heart-breaking* to me'. More to his liking were the countless 'tributes' which Forster observed pouring 'upon its author daily, all through that Christmas time' from fans testifying what an extraordinary book this was, 'to be kept on a little shelf by itself'.

In its short form the *Carol* is a miracle of compression, and compression is partly how it works. Much is crammed into its small space. Full to bursting with things, food, people, emotions, its prose overflows on the most unlikely provocation. Take the introduction of Scrooge:

> Oh! But he was a tight-fisted hand at the grindstone, Scrooge! a squeezing, wrenching, grasping, scraping, clutching, covetous, old sinner! Hard and sharp as flint, from which no steel had ever struck out generous fire; secret, and self-contained, and solitary as an oyster. The cold within him froze his old features, nipped his pointed nose, shrivelled his cheek, stiffened his gait, made his eyes red, his thin lips blue; and spoke out shrewdly in his grating voice. A frosty rime was on his head, and on his eyebrows, and his wiry chin. He carried his own low temperature always about with him; he iced his office in the dog-days, and didn't thaw it one degree at Christmas.
>
> (Stave I)

All those adjectives at the beginning proclaim a profligacy with language in exuberant contrast to Scrooge's meanness with money. Apostrophe, exclamation, simile, and metaphor: Dickens piles up his figures of speech and then pauses to enjoy the extended fancy of Scrooge's creation of his own micro-climate.

This is the most emotionally expressive of all Dickens's works, with its extremes of happiness and hardship, its tears of laughter and sorrow, its larger-than-life character responses, its abundance of vitality. Scrooge is no passive miser. Mr 'Bah Humbug!' is an energetic hater with his pantomime crossness: '"Every idiot who goes about with 'Merry Christmas' on his lips, should be boiled with his own pudding, and buried with a stake of holly through his heart"' (Stave I). Everything is animated, even the stuff on the market stalls: 'ruddy, brown-faced, broad-girthed Spanish Onions, shining in the fatness of their growth like Spanish Friars, and winking from their shelves in wanton slyness at the girls as they went by', and French plums blushing 'in modest tartness from their highly-decorated boxes' (Stave III).

Jollity abounds, but the *Carol* also bears a sterner message as befits its genesis. Scrooge's conversion from callous Malthusianism—are there no workhouses, are there no prisons, he asks—comes not because he is made aware of the two children Ignorance and Want, but because he is made aware of himself as a child. The Ghost of Christmas Past carries Scrooge back to his childhood, and 'his poor forgotten self as he used to be' (Stave II). The lesson he must learn in this parable of memory (Dickens is not quite ready for his own memory work, which would come at the end of the 1840s) is to open the way back to the 'self' forgotten by himself as well as by others. Memory unlocks tears, recaptures the emotions of childhood. Back to childhood, and into the town. Where city-dweller Mr Pickwick had to go to the country for his traditional Yuletide, the *Carol* is Christmas for city workers. Wassailing in feudal halls is modernized into Mr Fezziwig's office party.

The emotional temperature of the *Caro*l is bolstered by the manner of its telling: its orality. This is a tale designed to be read aloud, with a strong presence for the narrator. 'You will permit me to repeat', he says early on, as if engaging us in friendly conversation. His style is characterized by 'Oh!'s and exclamation marks, he explicitly installs himself by the reader's fireside 'close to you... in spirit at your elbow'. Dickens took the hint himself. The *Carol* was his first public reading in 1853 and his most popular, right up to his last reading in March 1870. From the moment it was published it was recognized as in a class of its own—a 'national benefit' in Thackeray's view, 'and to every man and woman who reads it a personal kindness'. The novelist Margaret Oliphant agreed that when it appeared 'it moved us all... as if it had been a new gospel', though she later decided it promoted only 'the immense spiritual power of the Christmas turkey'.

Turkey power, emotional energy, and accommodating elasticity have combined to fuel more retellings, adaptations, and reworkings than perhaps any other text in history. President F. D. Roosevelt read it aloud to his family every Christmas Eve; and every Christmas in the twenty-first century still embraces countless versions, public and private, amateur and professional. Mickey Cratchit and Scrooge McDuck, Muppets, Smurfs, Flintstones, Sesame Street, Dr Who, Batman, Barbie, Blackadder, and an All Dogs version have all joined the party; it has been performed in many languages, including Klingon. Dickens himself maintained the field with four more Christmas books in the ensuing years. After that, *Household Words* and *All the Year Round* featured Christmas numbers with stories written and commissioned by Dickens.

In his later fiction Christmas becomes more complicated. Christmas dinner at the beginning of *Great Expectations* is torture to young Pip. He is picked on by the adults, and guilty and apprehensive after stealing food to give the escaped convict Magwitch. This contraband becomes an alternative Christmas dinner, blessed by Joe. '"God knows you're welcome to it,"' he tells the recaptured Magwitch (Chapter 5). '"We don't know what you have done, but we wouldn't have you starved to death for it, poor miserable fellow-creature.—Would us, Pip?"' By the end of his life Dickens felt hostage to the brand he had created, complaining to his friend Charles Fechter: 'I feel as if I had murdered a Christmas number years ago (perhaps I did!) and its ghost perpetually haunted me.' But he could not let go, partly because it represented in distilled and iconic form the values he celebrated: the worship of home, fireside, and domesticity.

In his Company

Being in his company: this seems to be the motor driving all the business around Dickens and his characters, a motor fuelled by Dickens's own superabundant energies. He himself wanted and needed company; he preferred not to dine alone if possible. His characters were company to him; he told Forster it made him 'very melancholy' to leave them at the end of a novel. He expressed his relationship with his readers in social terms: the Prefaces attached to the final double-numbers of his novels favour gestures of friendship and neighbourliness. The author of *Nicholas Nickleby* 'flatter[s]' himself that his readers 'may miss his company at the accustomed time' now the book is finished; the Prefaces to *Bleak House* and *Little Dorrit* both end with the salutation 'May we meet again!'

From the 1850s onwards Dickens's public readings converted that virtual meeting into actuality. He revelled in being able to see his readers as he moved them to laughter and tears; he was reaping the rewards of that 'personal affection for me' which so sustained him, and to which he frequently referred. In the troubled year of 1858, having trampled on his circle of family and friends, he embarked on a frenetic series of readings and told Miss Coutts: 'I consider it a remarkable instance of good fortune that it should have fallen out that I should, in this Autumn of all others, have come face to face with so many multitudes.'

On the page, part publication sustains the friendship over time. This is no short-term encounter; the reader is bound into a long-term alliance, which could be interactive as readers wrote in and Dickens responded. 'N.B. I put Flora into the current No.' of *Little Dorrit* to please you, he told the ailing Duke of Devonshire in 1856. And from the start, enjoying his novels was often a collective experience. Forster recalled the charwoman who lodged at a snuff-shop where,

> on the first Monday of every month there was a Tea, and the landlord read the month's number of *Dombey*, those only of the lodgers who subscribed to the tea partaking of that luxury, but all having the benefit of the reading.

From charwomen to dukes, Dickens's appeal was seen to be cross-class and all-inclusive from the start. 'All classes read Boz', noted a reviewer as early as 1837. 'Mr Popular Sentiment', sneered the novelist Anthony Trollope. But in his obituary he acknowledged Dickens as the people's novelist: 'Wherever English is read these books are popular from the highest to the lowest.'

If the merchandizing was there from day one—*All the Year Round* perfume in June 1859, made by Rimmel within two months of the magazine's inception and 'Dedicated to Charles Dickens (with his kind permission)'—so too was the conviviality. Even to such a sombre novel as *Little Dorrit*, readers could sing and dance along, with *Little Dorrit* serenades, ballads, and polkas. The singing and the selling both survive in strength today: all the Dickens pubs and cafes attempting to monetize the aura of good cheer. He and his characters have been on stamps, coins, and banknotes, on medicine bottles, pincushions, and matchboxes, on playing cards, cigarette cards, and Christmas cards, on tea and biscuits, and on mugs by the million (see Figure 7).

Communality prevails, in the marketing as in the multifarious face-to-face events, whether commercial or scholarly, local or international. Dickens World, the Dickens Universe,

Figure 7 *Late-nineteenth/early-twentieth-century porcelain and fabric pincushions representing an odd assortment of Dickens characters. Dickens memorabilia take quirky shapes and forms.*

and Dickens Project, the Dickens days, walks, parades, fairs, and festivals are all ploys to be in his charismatic company. Costuming often appeals. His characters offer strong outlines to explore and play at: license to become the spoiler of the feast as well as its host, Scrooge and Miss Havisham as well as Mr Pickwick.

Founded in 1902, the Dickens Fellowship aimed to unite Dickens lovers 'in a common bond of friendship' and to campaign against the 'social evils' that concerned him. The Fellowship—the choice of name speaks for itself—is unusual in its cross-over between the academic and non-academic. The branches are autonomous, and each has its own identity. The scrapbooks of cuttings and ephemera compiled by the Fellowship during most of the twentieth century and now at the Charles Dickens Museum in London testify to the charms of topography. Walking his terrain has been popular since Dickens's own time. While visiting friends in Norwich, Thackeray suggested going a further twenty miles to see where the Peggottys lived in Yarmouth. Being in the same place as Dickens, having his characters with you. In 1916 Ernest Shackleton's band of stranded Antarctic explorers called the upturned boat they used as shelter Peggotty Camp.

As befits Dickens's own contradictoriness, commemorations of him ran into controversy before he was in his grave. His will could not have been clearer: 'I emphatically direct that I be buried in an inexpensive, unostentatious, and strictly private manner.' So his family made arrangements for a churchyard in a quiet Kent village. Then they were invited to inter him in a plot at Rochester Cathedral. But after an editorial in *The Times* proposed Westminster Abbey, a private funeral was conducted there. His grave in Poets' Corner was left open for two days and filled up with flowers brought by thousands of fans. The argument over whether his will proscribed all statues and memorials trundles on. From the outset, biography dealt in revelation, sensation, and scandal. John Forster's *Life of Charles Dickens* (1872–74) was structured into the twelve books of classical epic; but behind the public success was now revealed the debtors' prison, the blacking factory, the traumatized child. Forster did, though, withhold Ellen Ternan, despite her prominence in the will which he reproduces. Subsequent biographies have brought her back into the picture.

Global

Before the news of Dickens's death 'even reached the remoter parts of England' it had, Forster wrote in his biography, 'been flashed across Europe; was known in the distant continents of India, Australia, and America; and not in

English-speaking communities only, but in every country of the civilised earth, had awakened grief and sympathy'. Dickens himself, for all his associations with the metropolitan, had the habit of looking outwards and detested chauvinistic jingoism. He learned French and Italian as an adult, travelled and lived in Europe, visited North America, and contemplated a reading tour of Australia. He sent his sons to Australia and India. His characters range the world. Bob Sawyer and his pal Benjamin Allen go to India at the end of *Pickwick Papers*; Arthur Clennam arrives back from China at the beginning of *Little Dorrit*; Helena and Neville Landless come from Sri Lanka at the beginning of *Edwin Drood*. Businessmen, inventors, convicts, hopeful venturers, ne'er-do-wells, black sheep, and economic failures, all go or are sent abroad.

The novels themselves went global early in their lives, thanks to new developments in mass culture and communications. Annoyed though Dickens was by all the instant pillaging in these pre-international copyright times, the immediate access garnered huge audiences. By the 1860s his magazine *All the Year Round* had an authorized American publisher who could boast 'the largest circulation of any similar publication in the world', and for its serialization of *Great Expectations* 'in this country alone more than three million readers'. He was cherished in the remotest places. Bret Harte's 1870 poem 'Dickens in Camp' depicts miners in the 'dim Sierras' clustering round the 'roaring camp-fire' spellbound by readings from 'the Master': 'Their cares dropped from them like the needles shaken/From out the gusty pine.'

A cheering companion, Dickens quickly came to signify more widely, to represent and create a type of Englishness. This he now reflects back to the twenty-first century, so that Dickens, Englishness, and Victorian become catch-all synonyms for all that is loved or hated about the nineteenth century—those extreme oppositions again. In this century his portrait and the cricket match at Dingley Dell from *Pickwick Papers* have been on Bank of England ten-pound notes. Historians like to use him as a lens through which to identify Victorianism or Englishness, while castigating him for inaccuracy.

Dickens's role as a global signifier for Englishness, for better or worse, has had inescapable ramifications across its former colonies. On one hand he could be home transplanted for settlers in faraway countries. By 1838 a printer in Tasmania had published an edition of *Pickwick Papers*. Pickwick parties were thrown on Kangaroo Island (off the coast of South Australia), and men from sheep stations in the outback gathered to hear *Nicholas Nickleby* read around the campfire. They named calves and puppies after its characters. On the other hand he was also the heavy-handed tool of Empire itself. As bearer of the imperial culture he was bound to have a mixed reception. Introduced by colonial authorities into India, his books could find themselves discarded in favour of the less canonized Marie Corelli or W. H. Ainsworth. But he could still speak for the oppressed. A century later in South Africa, radicals mounted a revolutionary *Tale of Two Cities* in black townships. And his influence persisted for generations of writers, who were often compared to him and sometimes dubbed his successors.

Decolonization has entailed many rich and complex dialogues with Dickens, such as Peter Carey's *Jack Maggs* (1997) and Lloyd Jones's *Mister Pip* (2007). Such mixed messages match the contradictions in Dickens's fiction, where the empire features both as dumping ground for misfits and as cornucopia of splendid things ripe for the taking. This is Mr Dombey's view:

> The earth was made for Dombey and Son to trade in, and the sun and moon were made to give them light. Rivers and seas were formed to float their ships; rainbows gave them promise of fair weather; winds blew for or against their enterprises; stars and planets circled in their orbits, to preserve inviolate a system of which they were the centre. Common abbreviations took new meanings in his eyes, and had sole reference to them. A.D. had no concern with anno Domini, but stood for anno Dombei—and Son.
>
> (Chapter 1)

Dickens mocks Dombey's hubris. The echoes of the first chapter of Genesis suggest his blasphemous substitution of capitalist for spiritual and religious value; by the last sentence Dombey has replaced God. But were Dickens's own business instincts that different?

Dombey and Son also has one of Dickens's rare portrayals of a colonized subject. Major Bagstock has been in the Indian Army and employs a nameless servant, referred to as 'the Native', whom he treats cruelly. Where Dickens's sympathies lie, as with the American slaves in 1842, is clear. So his *Household Words* article on 'The Noble Savage' in 1853 seems surprising in its hostility. 'To come to the point at once,' Dickens begins defiantly, 'I beg to say that I have not the least belief in the Noble Savage. I consider him a prodigious nuisance, and an enormous superstition.' And so on in similar choleric vein for the length of the essay. The racism with which he has been charged by modern critics looks amply justified. But Dickens's attitudes to race are more nuanced and shifting than such criticism might suggest. The 'Noble Savage' essay, for instance, is primarily targeted at the show of 'Zulu Kaffirs' currently drawing the London crowds, and which Dickens felt to be bogus—the Native Americans on show a few years earlier had turned out to be from the East End of London. It is the performance and the caricature which infuriate him.

Four years later, however, with the First Indian War of Independence (known to Victorians as the Indian Mutiny) in 1857, Dickens's attitudes to race found sudden, strong, and momentary expression. His son Walter was fighting in the East Indian Army, reports of Indian atrocities were appearing in the British press, and Dickens joined in the wave of hysteria and denunciation. 'I wish I were Commander in Chief in India', he wrote in a private letter to Angela Burdett Coutts, claiming he would 'do my utmost to exterminate the Race upon whom the stain of the late cruelties rested . . . and raze it off the face of the Earth.' For public consumption he collaborated with Wilkie Collins on the story for the Christmas number of *Household Words*, 'The Perils of Certain English Prisoners'. Transposed to a 'very small English colony' off the coast of Belize and facing down bloodthirsty pirates rather than sepoys, Dickens's cast of valiant sailors and steadfast women were planned, he told Miss Coutts, 'in the hope of commemorating . . .

some of the best qualities of the English character that have been shewn in India'. Thereafter, observes the critic Grace Moore, 'a growing belief in the inferiority of non-white races' never left him, though he was never again so outspoken.

Reception

Wherever Dickens has been read—and that must be most countries—he has accrued particular meanings. In Europe, Michael Hollington discerns a common pattern: 'initial joyful discovery', then 'reaction and partial rejection, followed again by rediscovery in the context of Modernist art and the revaluation of alternatives to "Classic Realism"'. The first translation to appear was of *Pickwick* into German in 1837. French *Pickwick* was next, in 1838. By 1840, translations of Boz sketches had appeared in Czech and Polish; *Oliver Twist* was out in Danish and Italian, and *Nicholas Nickleby* in French. More European translations followed: Dutch, Norwegian, Hungarian, Romanian, Swedish, Portuguese, and Spanish by 1850; Greek, Bulgarian, and Icelandic by 1860; Croatian and Finnish by 1870, and Georgian, Catalan, Estonian, Slovak, Lithuanian, and Latvian by the turn of the century.

From the end of the 1830s he was being translated into Russian, where he exerted an unprecedented impact on the giants of nineteenth-century Russian literature: Tolstoy, Dostoevsky, Gorky, Gogol, and Turgenev. The English critic Henry Gifford, quoted by Michael Hollington, explains why. 'It was the primitive, the poetic and myth-working element in his imagination that gained Dickens an entry to Russian literature as if by an underground passage, so that he occupied it from the inside.' Unlike other countries which preferred his earlier fiction, Russian readers looked to the later darker novels, to the social critic with pity for the victims of injustice, and later to Dickens the democrat. Beyond Europe, Dickens has been popular in China since he was translated in the early twentieth century. He has in turn been celebrated as social crusader, rebuked for his bourgeois ideology during the Cultural Revolution, and applauded for his representatives of street folk. *Orphan in the Foggy City* was the title under which school-children met *Oliver Twist*, and Dickens is still considered influential on Chinese views of Britain.

In his home country his stock has risen, fallen, risen again. He may have ascended to Westminster Abbey on his death, but the popular-entertainer smear stuck, to deny him serious critical status. Consigning all Victorians to the dustbin, the early-twentieth-century Bloomsbury group did not make an exception for Dickens. Working-class readers never deserted him. He was, according to book historian Jonathan Rose, the most widely stocked novelist in Welsh miners' libraries, and was prominent on the lists of Labour MPs' favourite reading in 1906. In Rose's view, 'Dickens's most important gift to the working classes was the role he played in making them articulate. He provided a fund of allusions, characters, tropes and situations that could be drawn upon by people who were not trained to express themselves on paper.' Prisoners polled for a Home Office report in 1911 also ranked him highly. And there was a surge of popularity during the First

World War, as Dickens was felt to speak for the common man fighting for the decencies of humanity. He was read and performed in the trenches (some of them German), and adapted for stage and film at home. For his literary stock to rise, he had to wait until the 1940s. Appraisals by Edmund Wilson in America, and by George Orwell and Humphry House in Britain, foregrounded a more complex picture and kick-started the process. New developments in literary criticism have found Dickens congenial to analysis by post-structuralist and Foucauldian critics, and to approaches in post-colonialism and gender studies.

Translated, adopted, and adapted, Dickens has become a global language. The novels have proved themselves elastic. They are resilient to borrowings, open to conversations, hospitable to prequels and sequels. And where Dickens went himself with the adaptations he made for his sensational public readings (see Figure 8), the rest of the world has followed: with dramatizations, versions for film and television, comic and graphic novelizations, Japanese manga versions, children's pop-up versions, spoofs and take-offs, renditions in dance and visual art, in clay, china, and metal.

Unsurprisingly, radio and television have done Dickens proud. He has rarely been off the radio since a reading of 'Barkis is Willin' in 1924; he has been on television since a BBC version of *Pickwick Papers* in 1938. One of the most successful twenty-first-century versions was the 2005 BBC *Bleak House*, broadcast twice weekly in one hour-long episode and fourteen half-hour episodes with suspense endings. Serialization can accommodate Dickens's pace and technique, but fidelity to the original is not the point, as

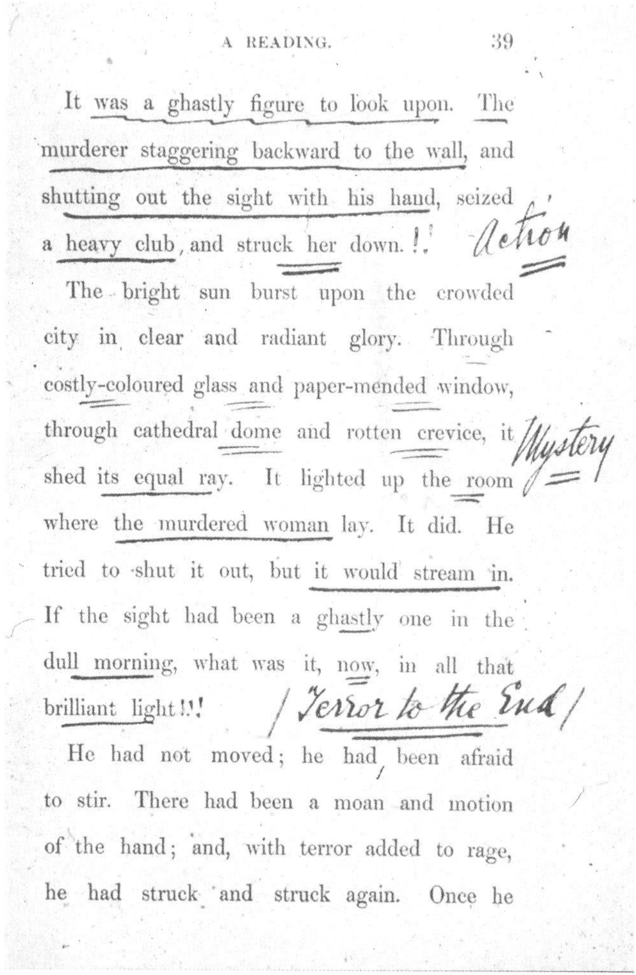

A READING. 39

It was a ghastly figure to look upon. The murderer staggering backward to the wall, and shutting out the sight with his hand, seized a heavy club, and struck her down. !! Action

The bright sun burst upon the crowded city in clear and radiant glory. Through costly-coloured glass and paper-mended window, through cathedral dome and rotten crevice, it shed its equal ray. It lighted up the room where the murdered woman lay. It did. He tried to shut it out, but it would stream in. If the sight had been a ghastly one in the dull morning, what was it, now, in all that brilliant light!!! Mystery

/ Terror to the End /

He had not moved; he had been afraid to stir. There had been a moan and motion of the hand; and, with terror added to rage, he had struck and struck again. Once he

Figure 8 A page from 'Sikes and Nancy', Dickens's adaptation of Nancy's murder in *Oliver Twist*. He recited from memory but carefully prepared a prompt copy, complete with melodramatic annotations.

the BBC's 2016 twenty-part serial *Dickensian* demonstrated. It brought together more-or-less well-known characters from different novels all now living on the same streets. Scheduled for early evening viewing, at times associated more with soap-opera rather than classic serial, *Dickensian* took on Dickens in the spirit of play, and exemplified the general principle of joyful appropriation at work throughout the Dickens business.

By the time of his bicentenary in 2012 Dickens could be celebrated as both mass and literary phenomenon. The accent was more self-consciously democratic and global than the 1912 celebrations, and able to be more interactive. The British Council sponsored a Global Readathon, comprising five-minute readings from twenty-four countries over twenty-four hours. It also invited creative responses to *Sketches by Boz*, with writers, artists, and photographers documenting their own rapidly changing cities. As for 'Dickensian' the adjective: it retains its literary resonance. Novelists are praised for their Dickensian scope, complexity of plot, and range of emotions as well—of course there is a downside—as admonished for their Dickensian sentimentality or reliance on coincidence. But the adjective has escaped the bounds of his books to roam the diversity of public discourses. The 'Dickensian world of decimated public services' was recently decried in a British parliamentary debate on spending cuts, while the 'Dickensian attitude... of forward Victorian thinking' was being advocated for engineering projects stalled by planning problems.

Dickens has been and always will be bigger than his books, as their spirits overflow into the conduits of communal affect. In his 1913 autobiographical essay 'A Small Boy and Others', Henry James described Dickens as 'the great actuality of the current imagination'. He is still current in our twenty-first-century imaginations, a novelist different in kind from all others. In 1908, G. K. Chesterton hailed him as 'a human event in history; a sort of conflagration and transfiguration in the very heart of what is called the conventional Victorian era'. That conflagration is still alight today.

TIMELINE OF DICKENS'S LIFE AND MAJOR WORKS

1812	Born in Portsmouth.
1815–22	Family moves to London, Chatham, and back to London.
1824	Sent to work in blacking warehouse; father imprisoned for debt in Marshalsea prison.
1825	Leaves blacking warehouse and goes back to school.
1827	Starts work as a solicitor's clerk.
1829	Works at Doctors' Commons as a shorthand reporter.
1830	Falls in love with Maria Beadnell.
1831	Reporter for *The Mirror of Parliament.*
1832	Parliamentary reporter on *The True Sun.*
1833	First story, 'A Dinner at Poplar Walk', published in *Monthly Magazine.*
1833–36	*Sketches by Boz*, published individually in magazines and newspapers, first collected 1836.
1834	Reporter for *The Morning Chronicle*; moves into own lodgings; meets Catherine Hogarth.
1836	Marries Catherine Hogarth; leaves *The Morning Chronicle*; meets John Forster.
1836–37	*The Pickwick Papers*, nineteen monthly numbers.*
1837	Editorship of monthly *Bentley's Miscellany*; birth of first child, Charley; moves to 48 Doughty Street; sudden death of Mary Hogarth.

1837–39	*Oliver Twist*, twenty-four monthly instalments in *Bentley's Miscellany*.
1838	Visits Yorkshire schools with Hablot K. Browne (Phiz); birth of second child, Mary (Mamie).
1838–39	*Nicholas Nickleby*, nineteen monthly numbers.*
1839	Resigns editorship of *Bentley's*; birth of third child, Katey; moves to Devonshire Terrace, Regent's Park.
1840	Editorship of weekly magazine, *Master Humphrey's Clock*.
1840–41	*The Old Curiosity Shop*, forty weekly instalments in *Master Humphrey's Clock*.
1841	*Barnaby Rudge*, forty-two weekly instalments in *Master Humphrey's Clock*; *Master Humphrey's Clock* concluded; birth of fourth child, Walter.
1842	Visits America with Catherine; *American Notes*, 2 volumes.
1843	*A Christmas Carol*, one volume (December).
1843–44	*Martin Chuzzlewit*, nineteen monthly numbers.*
1844	Birth of fifth child, Francis; takes family to Italy; *The Chimes*, one volume (December).
1845	Birth of sixth child, Alfred; *The Cricket on the Hearth*, one volume (December).
1846	Edits *The Daily News*, 21 January to 9 February; takes family to Switzerland, then Paris.
1846	*Pictures from Italy*, partially as 'Travelling Letters' in *The Daily News*, 1846, one volume; *The Battle of Life*, one volume (December).
1846–48	*Dombey and Son*, nineteen monthly numbers.*
1847	Birth of seventh child, Sydney; helps establish Urania Cottage in Shepherd's Bush.
1848	*The Haunted Man*, one volume (December).
1849	Birth of eighth child, Henry (Harry).

1849–50	*David Copperfield*, nineteen monthly numbers.*
1850	Editorship of weekly journal *Household Words*; birth of ninth child, Dora.
1851	Dora dies, aged 8 months; moves to Tavistock House.
1851–53	*A Child's History of England*, thirty-nine weekly instalments in *Household Words*.
1852	Birth of tenth child, Edward (Plorn).
1852–53	*Bleak House*, nineteen monthly numbers.*
1853	First public readings, *A Christmas Carol* and *The Cricket on the Hearth* in Birmingham.
1854	*Hard Times*, twenty weekly instalments in *Household Words*.
1855–57	*Little Dorrit*, nineteen monthly numbers.*
1856	Buys Gad's Hill Place, Kent.
1857	Meets Ellen Ternan.
1858	Separates from Catherine; first provincial reading tours.
1859	Final number of *Household Words*; begins editing weekly journal *All the Year Round*.
1859	*A Tale of Two Cities*, thirty-one weekly instalments in *All the Year Round*.
1860–61	*Great Expectations*, thirty-six weekly instalments in *All the Year Round*.
1860–69	*The Uncommercial Traveller*, 'Occasional Papers' for *All the Year Round*, first series collected in one volume in 1860.
1863	Death of son Walter in India.
1864–65	*Our Mutual Friend*, nineteen monthly numbers.*
1865	Railway accident in Staplehurst, Kent.
1867	Reading tour of America.
1868	American tour cut short due to ill health; farewell reading tour of UK.

1870	*The Mystery of Edwin Drood*, six of twelve projected monthly numbers.
1870	Dies of cerebral haemorrhage at Gad's Hill.

* Comprising twenty instalments, the last number incorporating two instalments.

FURTHER READING

GENERAL

The Forster Collection at the National Art Library (Great Britain) holds the manuscripts of most of Dickens's novels, plus printers' proofs, early editions, and artworks. Some of the manuscripts can be viewed online. See <www.vam.ac.uk/content/articles/n/national-art-library-forster-collection>. Dickens's two journals, *Household Words* and *All the Year Round*, are available online at <www.djo.org.uk>.

Two journals and an annual publication are devoted to Dickens: *The Dickensian* (published by the Dickens Fellowship, London), *Dickens Quarterly* (published for the Dickens Society by Johns Hopkins University Press), and *Dickens Studies Annual* (AMS Press). The Dickens Project—a consortium of major universities across the world—is based at the University of California at Santa Cruz.

Some of the best Dickens studies and commentaries have been produced by novelists: G. K. Chesterton, *Charles Dickens* (Methuen, 1906); George Gissing, *Charles Dickens: A Critical Study* (1898; Grayswood Press, 2004–05); Stefan Zweig, *Master Builders: A Typology of the Spirit*, Vol. 1, *Three Masters: Balzac, Dickens, Dostoeffsky*, trans. E. and C. Paul (Allen and Unwin, 1930); Graham Greene, 'The Young Dickens' (1950; *The Lost Childhood and Other Essays,* Eyre and Spottiswoode, 1951); George Orwell, 'Charles Dickens' (1939;

Collected Essays, Heinemann, 1961). Important reappraisals of Dickens in the mid-twentieth century include George Orwell (see above); Edmund Wilson, 'The Two Scrooges', *The Wound and the Bow: Seven Studies in Literature* (1941; Ohio University Press, 1997); Humphry House, *The Dickens World* (Oxford University Press, 1941); John Butt and Kathleen Tillotson, *Dickens at Work* (Methuen, 1957).

For more recent book-length reappraisals see: Rosemarie Bodenheimer, *Knowing Dickens* (Cornell University Press, 2007); John Bowen, *Other Dickens: Pickwick to Chuzzlewit* (Oxford University Press, 2000); John Carey, *The Violent Effigy, A Study of Dickens' Imagination* (Faber, 1973); Robert L. Patten, *Charles Dickens and his Publishers* (Clarendon Press, 1978).

The reception of Dickens's work has been well covered. A checklist of early criticism is provided in Kathryn Chittick, *The Critical Reception of Charles Dickens 1833–41* (1989; Routledge, 2015). *Dickens, The Critical Heritage*, ed. Philip Collins, is a good collection of early reviews and criticism; see also George H. Ford and Lauriat Lane Jr. (eds.), *The Dickens Critics* (Cornell University Press, 1961). Ashgate Studies in Publishing History has published *Charles Dickens's Great Expectations, A Cultural Life* 1860–2012 (2015) by Mary Hammond, and *Charles Dickens's Our Mutual Friend, A Publishing History* (2014) by Sean Grass.

Recent companions and collections of essays: *The Oxford Companion to Charles Dickens*, ed. Paul Schlicke (1999; Oxford University Press, 2011); *Palgrave Advances in Charles Dickens Studies*, ed. John Bowen and Robert L. Patten (Palgrave Macmillan, 2006); *The Cambridge Companion to Charles Dickens*, ed. John O. Jordan (Cambridge University Press, 2001); *Charles Dickens in Context*, ed. Sally Ledger and Holly Furneaux (Cambridge University Press, 2011); *A Companion to Dickens*, ed. David Paroissien (Blackwell, 2008).

A Library of Essays on Charles Dickens (series editor Catherine Waters, Ashgate, 2012) is a comprehensive six-volume collection of essays from the second half of the twentieth century and the twenty-first century: Vol. 1, *Dickens and the City*, ed. Jeremy Tambling; Vol. 2, *Dickens Adapted*, ed. John Glavin; Vol. 3, *Dickens, Sexuality and Gender*, ed. Lillian Nayder; Vol. 4, *Dickens and Childhood*, ed. Laura Peters; Vol. 5, *Dickens and Victorian Print Cultures*, ed. Robert L. Patten; Vol. 6, *Global Dickens*, ed. John O. Jordan and Nirshan Perera. The *Dickens Studies Annual* carries substantial review articles of recent Dickens scholarship.

CHAPTERS

1. More

British Film Institute, *Dickens Before Sound*, two-disc BFI DVD set curated by Michael Eaton, BFIVD526.

Jay Clayton, *Charles Dickens in Cyberspace: The Afterlife of the Nineteenth Century in Postmodern Culture* (Oxford University Press, 2003).

Percy Fitzgerald, *The History of Pickwick* (Chapman and Hall, 1891).

Juliet John (ed.), *Charles Dickens's Oliver Twist: A Sourcebook* (Routledge, 2006).

Robert L. Patten, *Charles Dickens and 'Boz': the Birth of the Industrial-Age Author* (Cambridge University Press, 2012).

Garrett Stewart, 'Dickens and Language', in *The Cambridge Companion to Charles Dickens*, ed. John O. Jordan (Cambridge University Press, 2001).

Daniel Tyler (ed.), *Dickens's Style* (Cambridge University Press, 2013).

2. Public and Private

Peter Ackroyd, *Dickens* (Sinclair-Stevenson, 1990).

Malcolm Andrews, *Charles Dickens and his Performing Selves: Dickens and the Public Readings* (Oxford University Press, 2006).

Mary Dickens, *My Father as I Recall Him* (Roxburghe Press, 1897).
Robert Douglas-Fairhurst, *Becoming Dickens: The Invention of a Novelist* (Belknap Press, 2011).
John Drew, *Dickens the Journalist* (Palgrave Macmillan, 2003).
John Forster, *The Life of Charles Dickens* (1872–74; J. M. Dent, 1927).
Jenny Hartley, *Charles Dickens and the House of Fallen Women* (Methuen, 2008).
Jenny Hartley (ed.), *The Selected Letters of Charles Dickens* (Oxford University Press, 2012).
Michael Slater, *Charles Dickens* (Yale University Press, 2009).
Michael Slater, *The Great Charles Dickens Scandal* (Yale University Press, 2012).
Claire Tomalin, *The Invisible Woman: The Story of Nelly Ternan and Charles Dickens* (Viking, 1990).
Claire Tomalin, *Charles Dickens: A Life* (Viking, 2011).

3. Character and Plot

Peter Brooks, *Reading for the Plot: Design and Intention in Narrative* (Harvard University Press, 1992).
Jane R. Cohen, *Charles Dickens and His Original Illustrators* (Ohio State University Press, 1980).
Michael Hollington, *Dickens and the Grotesque* (Croom Helm, 1984).
Juliet John, *Dickens's Villains: Melodrama, Character, Popular Culture* (Oxford University Press, 2001).
Valerie Purton, *Dickens and the Sentimental Tradition: Fielding, Richardson, Sterne, Goldsmith, Sheridan, Lamb* (Anthem Press, 2012).
Hilary M. Schor, *Dickens and the Daughter of the House* (Cambridge University Press, 1999).
Catherine Waters, *Commodity Culture in Dickens's Household Words, The Social Life of Goods* (Ashgate, 2008).

4. City Laureate

Matthew Beaumont, *Nightwalking: A Nocturnal History of London, Chaucer to Dickens* (Verso, 2015).

J. Hillis Miller, 'The Fiction of Realism: *Sketches by Boz, Oliver Twist,* and Cruikshank's Illustrations', in *Dickens Centennial Essays*, ed. Ada Nisbet and Blake Nevius (University of California Press, 1971).

Karl Ashley Smith: *Dickens and the Unreal City: Searching for Spiritual Significance in Nineteenth-Century London* (Palgrave Macmillan, 2008).

Alex Werner and Tony Williams, *Dickens's Victorian London* (Ebury Press, 2011).

5. Radical Dickens

John Drew, *Dickens the Journalist* (Palgrave Macmillan, 2003).

Sally Ledger, *Dickens and the Popular Radical Imagination* (Cambridge University Press, 2007).

Peter Merchant and Catherine Waters (eds.), *Dickens and the Imagined Child* (Ashgate, 2015).

D. A. Miller, *The Novel and the Police* (University of California Press, 1988).

Paul Schlicke, *Dickens and Popular Entertainment* (Unwin Hyman, 1985).

6. Dickensian

John Glavin (ed.), *Dickens on Screen* (Cambridge University Press, 2003).

Michael Hollington (ed.), *The Reception of Charles Dickens in Europe*, 2 vols. (Bloomsbury, 2013).

Juliet John (ed.), *Dickens and Modernity (Essays and Studies 2012)* (D. S. Brewer, 2012).

Laurence W. Mazzeno, *The Dickens Industry: Critical Perspectives 1836–2005* (Camden House, NY, 2008).

Grace Moore, *Dickens and Empire: Discourses of Class, Race and Colonialism in the Works of Charles Dickens* (Ashgate, 2004).

David Parker, *Christmas and Charles Dickens* (AMS Press, 2005).

Jonathan Rose, *The Intellectual Life of the British Working Classes* (Yale University Press, 2001).

Jerry White, 'Tapley in the Trenches: Dickens and the Great War', *The Dickensian*, 111/2 (Summer 2015).

INDEX